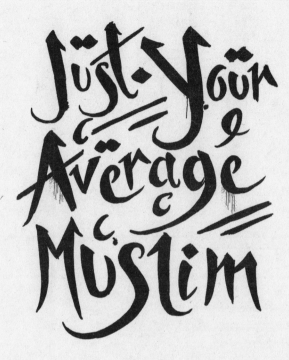

ZIA CHAUDHRY

Just Your Average Muslim

Published in 2015 by
Short Books, Unit 316, ScreenWorks, 22 Highbury Grove, N5 2ER

10 9 8 7 6 5 4 3 2 1

A CIP catalogue record for this book
is available from the British Library.

ISBN: 978-1-78072-248-1

Printed in Great Britain by CPI Group (UK) Ltd, Croydon, CR0 4YY

Cover design by Leo Nickolls

For Mikaal, Zaynadin and Hanaa.

May these words help you navigate your own paths in life.

CONTENTS

Introduction   9
1. The Seventies   19
2. Luck or blessings   41
3. Religion or science (or both)?   59
4. Have Muslims always been "thick"?   80
5. Or in need of anger management?   107
6. So who is the "enemy"?   135
7. And who are the silent majority?   161
8. How is it looking for the future, then?   185

Suggested further reading   214

Introduction

Despite 23 years of dealing with criminals on a daily basis, even my cynical mind was shocked when I saw the images of two men walking down a Paris street, in broad daylight, carrying assault rifles, which they proceeded to unload in the direction of unarmed civilians going about their business. Just when I thought that life couldn't get any worse, fate reminded me that, where Muslims are concerned, things can always be worse. It was a depressingly familiar feeling. The shock waves of the Charlie Hebdo killings reached around the world, and catapulted the usual Muslim-related debates back into the spotlight. The despicable actions of two deranged Frenchmen led to the by now familiar routine in which Muslims the world over are called upon to explain, denounce and apologise for their crimes.

What was somewhat less shocking was the usual parade of "experts" wheeled out to opine on Muslims, Islam, freedoms under threat, and so on and so on. One such expert from the USA betrayed the extent of his knowledge by referring to Birmingham (the English one, that is) as a Muslim city where non-Muslims feared to venture! It caused some amusement at the time, not least to the 75-odd per cent of Birmingham which is not Muslim, but mattered little, because the general public was by now gorging on a regular diet of horror stories about Muslims and their increasingly brazen bouts of violence, made all the worse by their proximity.

As I write this, a month after the events in Paris, the immediate levels of hatred may have subsided, but the dust seems to take longer to settle after each new atrocity. ISIS, IS, Daesh, or whatever else one chooses to call the lunatics of the Levant, may well be seeking to outdo themselves every few weeks with their latest instance of medieval thuggery, but at least their appalling antics are confined to the Middle East, where, of course, this kind of behaviour is all too common. But when our own civilised streets are under attack, that's a different matter. That is when we are all encouraged to summon our inner Churchill and bulldog spirits; that is when we start to recall the many sacrifices "we" made in order to defend the freedoms these savages are now trying to wrest from us. We have to make a stand as the last bastion of civilisation holding out against the return to the Middle Ages desired by these invaders.

The thing is, I'm not sure this seemingly straightforward depiction of "us" versus "them" is as accurate as we are led to believe. For a start, that dogged defending of our freedom benefited from a pretty significant contribution from the very people we are told now want to attack us – namely, the 400,000 Muslims who fought alongside us plucky Brits.

Then there is the fact that people are perfectly capable of holding multiple identities without it necessarily causing problems, as exemplified by the millions of Muslims happily settled in, and contributing to, non-Muslim countries. I'm afraid I have to speak up here, because I don't do the two camps thing. I'm proud to be British, but should not be made to feel guilty about objecting to certain government policies in a way which would not attract the slightest attention if I was the "average" white Englishman. I'm proud to be Muslim, too, but should not have to defend or explain, let alone sign up to, the many ridiculous things done in the name of my faith by people I have nothing in common with. Yet the media continues to paint a picture of two camps foresworn to be enemies for ever, seemingly oblivious to the damage being caused. Of course, sensational headlines sell newspapers. But at what cost? What about the sowing of seeds of mistrust within communities which are already struggling with unemployment, lack of opportunity and all the other uncertainties of modern life? Does that make for a healthy society? Surely it cannot be regarded as constructive to portray one community continually as "other", and demean it to such an extent that its youngsters come to regard themselves as different.

But let's put the question of the media's duty aside for the moment. Because while it is important, it is only one factor in a complex range of issues threatening good relations between Muslims and other faiths today – issues which I believe are key not just to improving inter-faith relations but to ensuring the well-being and prosperity of the world as a whole.

A few years ago, I experienced a sharp awakening about my responsibilities as both a Muslim and a British citizen, which I felt bound to address. It was – you will not be surprised to hear – around my 40th birthday. At a time when I thought I could have reasonably expected a degree of stability, certainty and confidence in the way my life was progressing, it suddenly seemed I was destined for anything but. Despite almost twenty years practising as a criminal barrister – which meant having to stand up and "perform" in court on an almost daily basis – here I was, racked with self-doubt, and feeling wholly unsure about where my life was heading. The career, which 20 years earlier had seemed to guarantee a rosy future, had been rocked by a series of moves by successive governments that had undermined the independent Criminal Bar to such an extent that many barristers with formerly healthy practices were now forced to pursue alternative career paths. The uncertainty surrounding work was accompanied by the onset of familial responsibilities. Although my record-breaking (at least for Muslims) resistance to tying the knot was a somewhat amusing achievement at the time, it seemed less funny now that I was a 40-year-old running around after two small children. The energy levels were diminishing, which, along with a rapidly expanding bald patch, served as a constant reminder that perhaps my best days were firmly behind me and that the future would involve little more than struggling to keep up with the children, pay the bills, and generally just get by (like most people, in fact). I began to reminisce about missed opportunities. My three monastic years at university may well have propelled me heavenward, but were not memorable for much else. Since then, I had lived off the kudos that came with being a barrister, but had hardly set the legal world ablaze with my talents; I feared that each day might hold the moment I would finally be "found out". Rather than diving enthusiastically into the pool of life, I had contented myself with paddling around the shallow end.

If all this pointed towards a mid-life crisis, I thought, then at least I could take heart from the fact that many a mid-life crisis has been the source of a rebirth or reinvention. As a Muslim, I found it not without relevance that even our beloved Prophet Muhammad (peace be upon Him) carried out his most significant work after the age of 40. So there was hope that perhaps the best was yet to come. There were undoubtedly things that I could do, and do well. For ten years or so, I had been delivering talks on Islam which, though hardly of the academic variety, had been well received: the years of addressing juries had clearly helped in enabling me to establish a rapport with an audience, and that soon emerged as my USP. It quickly became evident, too, that many audiences were not used to coming into contact with a fairly normal kind of guy who just happened to be a Muslim. This was important work, and was taking place at a time when it was very much needed.

After the tragic events of the 11th September 2001, Muslims faced a stark choice. They could keep their heads down and just try to live their lives, pretty much as the older generation had done since the 1960s. Alternatively, they could meet the challenges they faced head on, and attempt to address the concerns that much of the country now had about Islam and its adherents. Many people were questioning why we never heard from the "moderate" Muslims; others wanted to know if such people even existed. Islam was increasingly portrayed as an alien religion that had nothing to do with "our Judaeo-Christian values", and there was a sudden proliferation of so-called "experts" willing to opine on what Muslims really believed. Sadly, however, these experts were too often not Muslims, and in some cases had their own causes to advance.

It was against this background that I figured I could put my advocacy skills to no better use than to dispel myths about my faith, and so I began accepting any invitation to speak about Islam that came my way. Obviously, I regarded myself as a moderate Muslim – certainly as opposed to an extremist one – but I was also concerned about the definition of "moderate Muslim". Did it really refer to the overwhelming majority of Muslims I knew, who did not practise or condone intolerance and violence, or did it simply mean those who were compliant and not given to rocking any boats? These were questions that I needed to answer for myself, as well as for others.

For me, speaking about Islam meant developing good relations with those of other faiths. Unlike some of my fellow Muslims, I did not believe that people who followed other religions simply sat around in anticipation of one day receiving information about Islam. They were individuals and communities who had their own hopes and fears, talents and abilities, and, perhaps most importantly, their own humanity. Getting to know one's fellow human beings just for the sheer sake of it is not optional for Muslims but is, rather, a duty derived from the Quran itself. Happily, it was not exactly a new experience for me to speak to people outside the Muslim community. But perhaps even I underestimated just how much I could learn from them: I soon discovered that one of the incidental benefits of my interfaith work was having the opportunity to talk to people who actually *thought* about their religious beliefs. Believers who attempted to understand their faith and ponder its practical implications in their daily lives were notable by their absence in the Muslim communities with which I came into contact. Yet there was an abundance of such people on the inter-faith scene; becoming a part of that scene could only be an enriching experience. There seemed to be a depth to their religious understanding from which I felt some Muslims, myself included, should be learning lessons.

At a mundane level, ordinary Muslims are undoubtedly good at the ritual observance part of their faith. Many are deeply impressive when one looks at their sincere and genuinely held belief. These are qualities which cannot, and should not, be underestimated. However, we are not living in a religious age, but an age in which religious belief is constantly challenged, undermined, or simply sidelined. It is no longer sufficient to have genuine faith and engage in regular ritual observance if one's peer environment expects more. In a society which seeks answers, and is prepared to carry out the investigations which may unearth them, Muslim communities, perhaps more than most, can reasonably be expected to have their beliefs placed under the microscope. What we need to do, first and foremost, is ask whether Islam is simply intended for the moral instruction of individuals, or, whether it has a role to play in wider society. If, as suggested here, the latter is true, then we must try to understand our society and its needs. It is only then that we can begin to think about the message of the Quran, and consider how it may be put to practical use.

It may well be that Islam can offer a solution to the problems posed by materialist consumerism. There may be a spiritual void in people's lives which needs to be filled; there may be gross economic injustices which need alternative solutions to those which are currently being proposed, and which seem only to perpetuate the inequality. The Islam that may have answers to these problems, and others, is, in my view, not the Islam being practised by so many of its followers today. Although ritual observance is impressive and, indeed, necessary, it is a poor replacement for actually thinking about what one's faith means and how it can be adapted to modern life. Indeed, not thinking about one's faith runs contrary to many injunctions of the Quran itself.

Negotiations between faith and the realities of life, and subsequent adaptations and accommodations, were a common feature of early Islam. Since that "Golden Age", however, a rigidity has set in: Muslims are led to believe that all the necessary thinking has been done, and that now the path to salvation simply consists of following the existing rules. Little effort has been made to update, or reform, such rules, and, as a result, it is first and foremost Muslims themselves who suffer. It is a sad indictment of the level of thought taking place in many Muslim communities that the very mention of the word "reform" draws the ire of so-called scholars, and, therefore, in turn, the rest of the community. The constant revisiting of the faith which is necessary to its continued relevance, and which was so common in early Islam, is now confused with diluting the faith in order to please the non-believing West.

It seems that religion will not naturally wither away, as many of its critics have assumed. It was once considered inevitable that the evolution of enlightened thought would lead civilised people to discard the "primitive" religious baggage they had been carrying around for millennia. Religion was just another phase of development that humanity would outgrow on its evolutionary path, and a time would come when "pure" thinking, unfettered by superstition, would hold sway over the world. How shocking it must have been to those who held that view to witness the resurgence of religious thought in the latter part of the last century. It would perhaps have been understandable if such a resurgence was restricted to less developed societies which had failed to progress, and, therefore, had to conceal their shortcomings behind a veil of religion. Often, such societies are characterised by an aversion to any criticism of the way they are administered, and religion, therefore, provides a useful device for restricting such criticism and controlling populations who may be inclined towards independent thought. The fact remains, however, that this religious resurgence has not been limited to such underdeveloped societies but, rather, has taken a deep hold even in the liberal, educated, sophisticated West.

I believe that Islam has much to offer this world. Whether it comes from those born into the faith, or those who see it with the objectivity of onlookers, remains to be seen. What is plain, however, is that this faith will have to reconnect with its moral essence and become relevant again and, in order to do this, issues of reform will have to be addressed. The debate, which is presently restricted to highbrow academic circles, needs to be joined by all Muslims. And I hope that this book can play a small part in bringing some elements of that debate to the Muslim masses. Perhaps it can also contribute to reassuring non-Muslims that there is some thought taking place in the Muslim world and that it is of the constructive and enlightened variety. Perhaps all it can achieve is to shed some light on the life of one particular Muslim who is trying his best to reconcile his own faith with the needs of his modern lifestyle.

Whatever it may achieve, as ever, all praise is due to the Almighty, with only the mistakes belonging to us.

Zia Chaudhry, February 2015

1

The Seventies

If there is a car that sums up England in the Seventies, it is undoubtedly the Mark III Ford Cortina, as driven by DCI Gene Hunt in the original BBC TV series, *Life on Mars*. Some may argue that, in fact, the Consul/Granada, as featured in *The Sweeney*, best sums up the era. But Granadas were too big and posh, despite being used by Regan and Carter to capture all manner of London villainy. There will undoubtedly be supporters, too, of both the Capri and the Escort RS2000, made famous in *The Professionals*. But the boys of CI5 were clearly a cut above the rest of us – trainee James Bonds – and were, therefore, expected to drive flash motors. It is true that many a young lad growing up in the Seventies in Britain will have aspired to one day owning a Capri or an RS2000, but it was the Ford Cortina (grand-father of the Mondeo, for younger readers) which was most likely to have be owned by his dad (unless, of course, he happened to be Asian – but we shall come to that later).

The Cortina was the car of the ordinary British working class, and so, for many years, Ford felt it appropriate to make it look as plain and ordinary as its likely customers.

The original Mark I may have had a restrained elegance about it, but its successor could have been designed by any 12-year-old with a ruler. The Mark IV, which arrived in the Eighties, was proof that Ford could also draw upon the talents of primary school children; its preponderance of straight lines made even the Volvos of the day look alluringly curvaceous. But the Mark III was, quite simply, stunning. It had just the right combination of straight lines and curves to signify purpose and elegance, and none more so than the GXL model, circa 1973. Twin headlights gave it a sporting menace, and the initials themselves made it sound like it meant business. In the Eighties, Gene Hunt may well have said, "Fire up the Quattro", but ten years earlier he would have just uttered "GXL" to inspire his foot soldiers in their pursuit of the bad guys.

Perhaps the GXL impressed me most because my uncle drove one. White may well be the new black at the moment, but in 1976 it was just another boring colour for cars, and one that was likely to get very dirty very quickly given the general grubbiness of that decade. A white GXL, however, complete with black vinyl roof, was the ultimate in cool. And while every other Asian family we knew owned either a Toyota or a Datsun (now Nissan), my uncle was "rolling" in a Ford, complete with automatic transmission, which, in those days, was about as *Starsky and Hutch* as you could get. After a brief abdication of his responsibilities while he owned a green Morris Marina, he had returned to hero status.

Cruising the mean streets with my uncle in his white GXL provided me with some of my happiest moments that decade. The mean streets of where, exactly? Well, any glamour ends there, because we are not talking about the showbiz glitz of, say, 1970s London. In fact, we are not even talking about a city or even a major town up north. No Manchester or Liverpool just yet. Instead, the scene is set in a place called Brierfield, East Lancashire, situated between Burnley and Nelson, not far from Pendle Hill. Brierfield was a small place – even now its population is less than 10,000 – but to a six-year-old it might as well have been a big city. It was home to my immediate family, wider relations and many friends. One of my mother's brothers lived 50 yards in one direction; the other lived further afield, possibly even as far as 100 yards away. Street upon street of terraced houses gradually worked their way up the hill, stretching from the farms and the railway station at the bottom to the more "affluent" parts of town at the top. It seems ridiculous looking back on it now, but you could mark your social standing by how far up the hill you lived. At the time, we had managed to "progress" a good way up – in fact, we secured our social status in the community by being the furthest up the hill of all the town's Pakistani families. Progress indeed. (Funnily enough the Pakistani family who lived nearest to us had a similarly aspirational outlook, wanting to gain an education and make the most of the opportunities afforded to them in their adopted home. Their son was a pal of mine, but I had little idea then that he would end up marrying my sister over 20 years later, long after we had left the area. I was even less aware that he would go on to become Britain's first Muslim Member of the European Parliament.)

It was fitting that we lived all the way up there, given my father's role in the community.

Mohammad Din Chaudhry had arrived from Pakistan

in 1962 with nothing but a bag of clothes and a law degree from Peshawar University. Having spent a brief amount of time in London and Nottingham, he decided to move north, where work was guaranteed and property was cheaper, knowing that he would have to buy a house before calling over the rest of the family from their village in the north-east of Pakistan. In the Sixties, there were plenty of factories in Lancashire offering work, but this would only be a short-term measure. Having been the only person in his whole district in Pakistan to have gained any meaningful education, let alone graduate from university, my father was clearly capable of greater things. He was an only child and his mother had died when he was a very small infant. His father was one of three brothers who owned some land – not enough to make them very wealthy, but enough to command the most respect in their village. Of the three brothers, two worked the land while the third was in the army. It soon became apparent to my grandfather that his son had abilities that would be wasted if he were to remain farming the land. Besides, it was not strictly necessary, as my grandfather had a brother and nephews, all of whom were doing this work anyway. So he decided to let his son go and live with the third brother, whose army posting meant that he lived away from the village, in a town with a school. Fortunately, my father made the most of this opportunity. He excelled at school, and managed to go to university when everyone around him was resigned to a rural life requiring little in the way of formal education.

He obtained his law degree, and his intention, when he arrived in England, was to become a barrister, thereby following in the footsteps of Muhammad Ali Jinnah, the founder of Pakistan, and his inspiration, Muhammad Iqbal, the great poet of the Indian subcontinent. Grand ambitions for a talented man, but ambitions which did not make any allowance for the tuberculosis that hospitalised him for several months. When he re-emerged from hospital, a career at the Bar no longer seemed so inviting. It has always been a precarious existence and, for my father, newly arrived in the country and recovering from a serious illness, it simply posed too many problems – not least because it would have required regular attendance at the Inns of Court in London. He did, however, appreciate that he had to enter a profession, and so it was that he began to study to become a teacher.

In the Sixties, the Pakistani community in East Lancashire consisted almost entirely of single males who originated from villages in the Punjab area of Pakistan. They had initially come to England with the intention of working, sending money back home, and ultimately returning there themselves. They could not boast an education, but the jobs they took on did not require one. They were manual labourers, factory workers who divided their days into working shifts while out of the house, and sleeping shifts while in. I recall being told stories of how the terraced houses contained none of the luxurious but useless clutter we have become accustomed to today, but simply beds and wardrobes to fulfil the basic functions required. The beds were vacated for the day shift, only to be immediately occupied by those returning from a night's work. Although the intention was to send any money earned back home, these workers gradually decided to have their family members join them here, which meant spending money on property. Initially, it was other male family members who joined them, but soon wives were called over, too.

The process of sponsoring family members to bring them over, as well as plenty of other tasks necessary to simply getting by in England, required the filling out of official forms. This was not a task these young men were equipped for, and so they had to find someone who could help. Which is why my father's life at the time was divided between work, study, and providing translation services to those that needed them in order to cope with the paper-work. (On his death in 1999, one of my father's old friends came to pay his respects. I remembered him from my child-hood, but had not seen him for some 20 years following his move to Scotland. He fondly recalled how they would make arrangements to go out when they were not working. As he was the one with the car, he would call round to pick my father up. He would get frustrated, he said, because, just as they were about to leave the house, another person would arrive, asking that my father help him fill out a form. He would never refuse, so they were invariably delayed. Apparently there was only one other man in the locality who could assist with the filling out of these forms but, as he charged a fee, it was my father who was the more prevailed upon.)

By the late 1960s, my father had been joined by my mother and three of her brothers. Initially, they all lived together, but pretty soon my uncles bought their own homes, leaving space for the arrival into this world of myself and my two younger sisters.

My memory of the early Seventies is understandably vague, but I do remember being fascinated by cars from a very early age. Although even I suspected, and perhaps hoped, that I would grow out of it, this interest (or obsession) now looks like it will remain with me for the rest of my life. My mother reports incidents which even I cannot recall, such as the time one of my father's friends called round to see him and, finding that he was not at home, offered to take me for a ride in his car until my father returned. No sooner had he suggested this than I was in the passenger seat and we were off. After a while, my mother began to worry and, somewhat belatedly perhaps, realised that she did not, in fact, know this individual particularly well at all. Needless to say, she was panicking by the time my father returned. He calmly assured her that there was nothing to worry about. I was duly brought back safe and sound. Although I do not remember this particular incident, I do recall that my heroes at the time were any of my dad's friends who had cars.

The Pakistani community had already begun to evolve by the Seventies, and the very same men who started their lives in England as factory workers now began to display an entrepreneurial spirit that remains very much alive today. Although most of the people who had moved from Pakistan to East Lancashire were from a rural background, and, therefore, instinctively less inclined to become involved in business, some clearly recognised the opportunities on offer and saw that they could exert some control over their own fortunes. One popular business, which remains as attractive now as it was then, was mini-cabbing. Working for a mini-cab firm means you can work as many hours as humanly possible, have a greater control over your life, and get cash in your hand, and is perhaps, therefore, more attractive to immigrants than it is to others. It was certainly attractive to young Pakistani men in the Seventies who wanted to escape the monotonous shift work of the factories and mills, and they began to set up their own mini-cab firms. One such firm was Goldline Taxis, which was set up in Nelson around 1976. That was the year we moved away from the area, but the memory of that firm serves as a reminder of how the Pakistani community lived at the time.

It was set up by a Pakistani man who had the advantage of belonging to a family with an intriguing dynamic, combining humility and respect with *Godfather* levels of scheming and violence. He was the second oldest of four brothers; the eldest, a patriarchal figure, was one my father's best friends. This eldest brother had been involved in an accident at his workplace and lost a couple of fingers. Inevitably, he wanted to claim compensation, which required the filling out of official paperwork. So he approached my father for assistance. This was provided, as usual, in return for no remuneration. But, on this occasion, it was provided to someone who did not forget a favour.

Many people had their forms completed by my father then disappeared back to their everyday lives. But Muhammad Sharif was made of different stuff. He may have been completely uneducated, but he possessed a personality that commanded the respect of all who met him. Despite coming from a simple, rural background he had contacts in Pakistan which went all the way up to the higher echelons of government, and it was evident from the reactions he aroused in people that, although he spoke softly, it was always likely that there was a big stick not too far away. It would be unfair to suggest that violence played a large part in his daily life, but, as with many men of power, it was an option which was available to him in a way it simply was not for regular people. It was over a decade later, in the mid-Eighties, when he was shot dead in Pakistan, that I learned that such power often comes at the expense of making enemies en route.

To me he was an "uncle", a friend of my father's who was utterly gentle with children – and, indeed, anyone I saw him with. He was also an individual whose company my father seemed to particularly enjoy. I have vivid recollections of accompanying my father to Uncle Sharif's house in Nelson. It was a two-up, two-down terraced house that was occupied at the time by Sharif and one of his younger brothers. On the rare occasion that I visit such dwellings now, I am surprised at how small they really are. When I was a child, however, they were just normal houses. And some of them could certainly pack in the "uncles". I remember Uncle Sharif's house in particular because it seemed to be the place where the most uncles congregated. The tiny sitting rooms were full of smoke, although there appeared to be a respectful curtailing of the chain-smoking in the presence of my dad. Cups of tea and plates of food were brought through from the kitchen at appropriate intervals. The most abiding memory I have, though, was of the incessant conversation. Hours would pass as the men talked and talked. I was inevitably bored and restless, but I was never one of those children who fell asleep easily, preferring instead to remain constantly awake in case I might miss something (a trait which I seem to have passed on to my own children). Little did I realise that some of those conversations would remain with me for ever.

Our family belongs to the Gujjar caste. Although Islam is supposed to be egalitarian, with no preference afforded to one group over another, in reality this is an often-contravened ideal. According to the tenets of our faith, it is only our God-consciousness, or righteousness, which should distinguish us from each other. But life on the Indian subcontinent was not so clear-cut. There, Islam had to accommodate itself to the Hindu way of life, in which the caste system featured prominently. Thus, many aspects of Pakistani culture have just as much of an Indian Hindu flavour about them, as they do an Islamic flavour. Food, dress, language and the caste system all reflected the inter-woven lives of Muslims, Sikhs and Hindus on the subcontinent. Changing one's faith was a relatively straightforward matter compared to doing anything that might breach the limitations of the caste into which one was born. My father never made a big issue of it, but I still managed to glean that there was a great pride that we were born into the Gujjar caste rather than any other. (No doubt people from other castes feel the same way. It is probably a good thing that this particular feature of our culture is fading. After all, some may reasonably argue that we have enough to deal with without complicating our lives further with caste considerations.)

In East Lancashire in the 1970s, such caste loyalties still played a significant role. Unlike now, money did not seem to impress people particularly, and those who gathered at Uncle Sharif's house certainly did not talk about it. Material possessions did not seem to matter, either; all the conversations were about respect and honour. Most of the people who congregated there were Gujjar and, rightly or wrongly, felt their caste was the epitome of such qualities. Gujjars were said to be men of respect and valour, integrity and honesty (and perhaps a tendency to throw punches first and ask questions later). They were also relatively simple folk – a bit unreconstructed, actually, maybe even a bit "Yorkshire" (as for Gujjars from Yorkshire, well...). The conversations, therefore, consisted of many tales of Gujjar heroism, and some good-hearted mockery of friends who had the misfortune of being from other castes.

The one feature that stands out all these years later, however, is the relative absence of religion from those conversations. Nowadays it is an inescapable topic of conversation in Muslim households, often depressingly so given that religious issues rarely seem to be associated with good news these days. But back then being Muslim was almost incidental to being a Pakistani as far as outsiders were concerned, and to being a Gujjar as far as those within the community were concerned. The battles literally fought with the National Front were nothing to do with their "fear" of Muslims, as their equally repugnant BNP descendants today claim, but were simply because they fancied some "Paki-bashing". Amongst Muslims in that area there just did not appear to be any major discussion of global politics of the kind that so animates them today, which reflects the prevalent attitudes of that community.

The community was certainly a Muslim one, but in an almost "Christian" way. And just as Christians, as the common criticism has it, had turned their religion into a once-a-week ritual, so members of the Pakistani community of East Lancashire were happy to observe occasional religious rituals but not to let Islam inform the way they lived their daily lives. Perhaps this was partly because it was still a very new community on these shores. Most of the Pakistani inhabitants of Brierfield had arrived in the previous decade or so, and were still concerned with the basics of setting up home here – finding jobs, houses, schools, places to pray. But as nobody appeared to object to them practising Islam, there really was not much to get excited about on the religious front.

There were no hijabs or niqabs. Funny clothes and even funnier facial hair, at least on the men, did not cause outrage (although that may well have been because they were a common feature of the Seventies). There were no Members of Parliament who, now that they were no longer in need of Muslim votes, blubbered about feeling intimidated by the clothes that their female Muslim constituents wore (although, again, maybe Lancastrian politicians in the '70s were made of sterner stuff). Newspapers did not carry the now almost daily debates about whether Islam is compatible with "British values". It is tempting to think that perhaps this is because there were no international events in those days that thrust Muslims into the headlines in the way they do now. But that patently cannot be correct. The oil crisis of 1973 clearly had the Western world in a panic, and it was undoubtedly due to decisions taken by people who happened to be Muslims. But, unlike today, there was no pervading requirement that all Muslims in Britain should explain themselves (well, not in East Lancashire anyway).

My own initiation into the faith appeared to be taking the usual path: I was sent to mosque, aged about five, to take part in classes to learn how to read the Quran. The usual path was disturbed, however, when I returned home from my first lesson to announce that there was no way I was going back. I had been used to a fairly relaxed household, and seemed to be progressing well enough without anybody having to scare the life out of me. I was regarded as reasonably bright, and my father's personal interest in education meant that he was never going to leave mine to the school system alone. He tutored me and my sisters from an early age, and it soon became apparent that, out of the three of us, I needed the least supervision. It came as something of a shock, therefore, when I went to my first class at the mosque. For a start, despite my father's involvement in the community, I do not recall having many Pakistani friends at an early age, so I felt out of place as soon as I walked through the door. And the system of learning by rote, with the maulvi (imam) sitting at the head of the group, wielding a big stick, did not exactly fill me with a desire to master Arabic.

Upon hearing my announcement, my father understood that this particular style of "teaching" may not have suited me, so he was content for me to learn to read the Quran at home, with daily tuition from him or, more often, my mother. The happy result was that I managed to "finish" the Quran – i.e. read it from beginning to end in Arabic – by the age of six. By comparison, most of those who learned to read it at the mosque achieved the same by the age of 12. I clearly remember the achievement being regarded as an almost barmitzvah-like rite of passage, marked by proud celebrations. In those days, having one's children learn to read the Quran was the only real interest the Pakistani families around us displayed in Islam. In fact, I do not recall ever seeing the daily prayers being performed at anyone's house, including ours. Religion really did seem to be incidental to daily life.

All this was to change, however, after November 1976.

That was when we moved from our East Lancashire back-water to the city of Liverpool, which, although only 56 miles away, might as well have been the other end of the country. For the previous couple of years, my father had been working in Liverpool in a particularly satisfying job, teaching English to foreign students at Crown Street Language Centre. His routine of staying there during the week and returning home at weekends was only intended to be a temporary arrangement, but he soon realised that Liverpool was where he wanted to bring up his children. It was an astonishing decision at the time. After all, he would be moving away from all his family and friends to a place where he hardly knew anybody. Not only that, but he would be going from being a big fish in a small pond to quite the opposite. I can actually remember people trying to dissuade him, appealing to him by suggesting that the community would struggle without him.

As ever, he knew best. For a start, the community was now reasonably well established, and, in any event, all he had done for them was a bit of translating – hardly life or death stuff. More importantly, however, he had correctly assessed the relative merits of the educational facilities available to his children in Liverpool compared to those in Brierfield. He realised that if he stayed, his children *could* succeed, but it would be without the support of good schools and like-minded peers. In Liverpool, however, not only were there many good schools, but the Pakistani community was very different to that of East Lancashire. There were no textile mills, and the Asians who lived there were predominantly professionals or business people. The chances were that his children would have as their friends the children of educated people who valued education.

Although my father's surprising decision proved to be something of a masterstroke, it certainly did not seem like that to me and my sisters at the time. Liverpool was an alien world for us. We had become used to a very different kind of life in Brierfield, where we had only ever entered people's houses through their back doors. In Liverpool, not only did we learn to use the front door, but we also had to suffer the indignity of telephoning before we called round. Who on earth did these people think they were? They seemed to have something of a superiority complex; for the first time, we encountered the mutual appreciation society which was the world inhabited exclusively by Asian doctors. I had been brought up to call all adults either uncle or auntie, yet here I saw children referring to close family friends as Doctor so and so.

It was all very bizarre, impersonal and quite off-putting. It was also strange to have no Pakistani neighbours – and, indeed, no Pakistani families in the neighbourhood. Nothing seemed within walking distance here, unlike at our former home, where taking public transport was a rare occurrence. As we did not have a car at the time, any journey over a mile or two had to be by bus. We could only get to the mosque or the city centre by bus. My school was a good twenty-minute walk away, too, and once there I had to suffer the indignity of fellow pupils laughing at my accent and calling me a "woolly back".

We may initially have lacked the comfort of familiarity, but, thankfully, we also lacked many of the negative aspects of life in Brierfield. Being part of the large Gujjar community had its advantages – especially if your family was well regarded – but it also meant that people were always inter-fering in each others' business. Those who may have had a grievance with a family back in a village in Pakistan, for example, would carry on that grievance with relatives who lived in England. This often led to violence, particu-larly amongst Gujjars, who were not averse to exchanging blows. We children did not see any violence ourselves, but we were aware that it was never too far away. In one instance, someone did not take too kindly to my father providing advice to a particular individual, and decided to mark their displeasure one evening by sending a brick through the window. For us this was a rare occurrence – the only one that I am aware of, in fact – but I regularly heard stories about others getting into fights. The Gujjar taxi driver/drunken English passenger interface was a common refrain of Seventies Lancashire. This was an environment my father wanted to protect us from; futile clan grudges over village politics and scrapping with drunks was not the life he intended for us, and nor was it a life led by those we encountered in Liverpool. Strange though these new neighbours appeared, they seemed to get on with their lives without fighting with each other, and seemed more inter-ested in making a success of whatever it was that they did.

We are still talking about the late Seventies, of course – just three television channels (on our black and white telly), no "tinternet", and no obsession with fancy food – but pretty soon after our move to Liverpool I did begin to feel that it was a more advanced environment than the one I was accustomed to. It was a city, after all, and one which was inhabited by people who had jobs that did not involve them getting their hands dirty. Rather than constantly talking about what was happening in their village in Pakistan, they seemed more interested in discussing important topics; politics did not mean village politics, but what was happening in the world. General Zia's ascendancy to power in Pakistan, the hanging of his predecessor Zulfikar Ali Bhutto, the Russian invasion of Afghanistan and the now famous resistance of the Mujahideen – these were all new topics of conversation between my father and his friends. And the common thread that seemed to run through all these conversations was Islam. This, in part, was due to the nature of the subjects. General Zia had made it clear that he wanted a more "Islamic" Pakistan, unlike that of his predecessor – even if that meant having to oppose Shariah law, which he subsequently did. The Mujahideen resistance of the Russians by means of "jihad" was again a struggle couched in religious terms (and, in fact, wholly supported by an America whose media never tired of extolling the virtues of jihad, as long as it was against the Russians). Partly, also, the religious nature of the conversations reflected the people with whom they were conducted.

Recently, when reading Zia Sardar's excellent *Desperately Seeking Paradise*, I was astonished to discover a mention of Dr Ahmed Zaman Khan within the first few pages. I knew the man well; he was one of my father's best friends, and one of the first people we met upon moving to Liverpool. I did not anticipate that he would figure in a book by such a well-known Muslim writer, especially one whose views are of a more progressive and thoughtful nature – attributes which could not really be used to describe the dear Doctor. That, however, is exactly why he figures in the book. His "brand" of Islam was, and still is – despite some mellowing over the years – one of absolutes, black or white, right or wrong. In the early 1970s, when Sardar first met him, he was at his peak in terms of fitness, loudness and zeal. It was entirely understandable that Sardar would use him as an example of the nature of Muslim practice in Britain in the early days, and to demonstrate to what extent, if any, it had developed from that position since.

Dr Ahmed Zaman Khan was a dentist, but the title Dr Zaman was how he was, and still is, known. He was a larger than life character in more ways than one – a giant of a man, whose main interests were eating, weight training and Islam. As a young man in Pakistan he had been something of a boxer, and it was only later that he somehow, to his own surprise, managed to navigate the academic path to dentistry. The wonderful dentition with which I have been blessed has meant that my experience of Dr Zaman's dentistry skills was happily brief, but not everyone was so lucky. The fact that he only had one eye may, arguably, have impacted on his practice, and he himself joked about how his patients would regularly leave his surgery and go straight to the solicitor's next door in order to seek legal redress for his haphazard rearranging of their teeth.

Dr Zaman certainly had a good sense of humour, and he was an utterly genuine and honest man. He was also one of the most hospitable people we knew, not only insisting that any visitor to his house stay for dinner, but also putting up many a visitor from abroad, for days, if not weeks on end. He would, at his own expense, take such visitors on tours the length and breadth of Britain. Which was all just as well, because sometimes it looked like he was going out of his way to start a fight. He would pointedly ask female Muslim patients why they were not wearing the hijab, making their visits to the dentist even more uncomfortable than usual. He would insist (perhaps forgetting the Quranic injunction that there is no compulsion in matters of faith) that any Muslim visitor to his house would join in when it was prayer time. It was rare that anyone refused the ex-boxer, whose generosity was matched by his temper. When others, including his closest friends, suggested to him that perhaps his interpretation of Islam was not the only one, he would often get so animated that it seemed blows were inevitable. Happily, that never occurred, but I recall the frustration of his guests who, try as they might, could not convince him that Islam did not forbid televisions. His logic was unique, however, and he would happily go from banning televisions one year to having several in his house a few years later. He would insist on the strict segregation of the sexes where there was any Muslim gathering, yet was more than content to go to supermarkets brimming with "infidel" housewives. Not surprisingly, he was very visible in late Seventies Liverpool, and played no small part in discussions involving Islam.

By this stage, the Muslim community in England was starting to find its feet, and, for various reasons, was beginning to consider actively its faith and the practice thereof. This was certainly more evident in Liverpool than in the towns of Lancashire, and it was clear by now, even to ten-year-old me, that Islam was going to play a significant role in my life whether I liked it or not. It was not just Dr Zaman: several other families banned television, too, due to the way they chose to practise their faith. That itself was manageable, but some of them were so stern and puritanical in their insistence on others joining in at prayer time that it was quite intimidating to visit them. It was many years before I could understand the reasons for these strictures, let alone summon up the courage to question the way they did things. The UK Islamic Mission was behind much of the zeal on display, as it was the major Islamic organisation, especially for the educated members of the older generation. It was hard to argue against much of the good work that it did, but the problem lay in the all-or-nothing approach to faith which many of its members adopted.

More recently, this organisation has been accused of being part of an international Saudi-funded Wahhabi network. The pejorative undertones this carries today are due to an overly simplistic view of what it stood for. It is true that the Mission may have had financial support from Saudi Arabia – which understandably meant that their stance would be one with a distinct Saudi flavour – but, more often than not, this manifested itself as religious orthodoxy rather than anything more sinister. It did not mean extremism as we know it today; there was not even a hint of violence. What it did mean was a puritanical approach to practising the faith, an approach which made little allowance for differences of culture and little effort to adapt to the practical realities of day to day life in a modern society. The necessity for such adaptation was not so clear at the end of the Seventies, when the Muslim community was pretty much left to its own devices. It was still a young community in Britain, and one whose children were only just beginning to get involved in the education system. It was only later, when these children faced the difficult task of balancing two parallel lives – their school friends inhabiting one, and their parents the other – that some of the more educated and thoughtful Muslim parents began to reconsider the way they practised their faith, realising that the traditions they had inherited from Pakistan, India, Yemen or wherever may not suffice for England.

My own family was yet to begin this thought process. My father ensured that his children were taught the basics of Islam, and, for the time being, that was enough. It was more important that we all received a good education – that was what would guarantee our "survival" in a modern society. My father played his part admirably, ensuring that his meagre teacher's salary could enable us to live in a decent part of the city, surrounded by good schools and good people. He was ably assisted by my mother who, like many other Pakistani mothers at the time, used to do sewing piecework, from home, to supplement the family income. Between them, they somehow managed to earn enough to move to a nicer house within a couple of years of our arrival in Liverpool. We would have a garden, a garage, and for the first time in our lives could escape the back yards and alleys that came with terraced houses.

My father's purchase of a nice semi-detached house clearly illustrated that he had absolutely no intention of keeping himself and his family in working-class surroundings, preferring instead the middle-class lifestyle that his colleagues enjoyed. We were sent to a nearby junior school, which served its purpose well (and, in fact, was recently brought back to my attention when I discovered that the former Attorney General Lord Goldsmith had also studied there). It was drummed into us from an early age that we must do well at school, and I, being the eldest, the brightest, and the only boy, felt the pressure weighing heavily on me from my junior school days. My real passion was still for cars, and I was disappointed that the first car my dad purchased was a sensible Datsun 120Y rather than something I could boast about at school. I realised that, to my father at least, cars came a distant second to academic achievement. A lot was expected of me and that pressure only intensified when the time came to apply to a secondary school.

2

Luck or blessings

In 1980, the Blue Coat was probably the best school in Liverpool, certainly as far as academic results were concerned. Thirty odd years later, not much has changed in that regard. It was a voluntary aided grammar school, which back then was mostly made up of day pupils, plus a few boarders. Its academic results were outstanding year in, year out, and my father had decided that this was the school I should be going to. The only problem was that entrance was competitive; to get in, I needed to "pass" an interview, and provide a recommendation from the head teacher of my primary school. I was reasonably bright, but it was a less than encouraging start when the exceptionally bright son of some family friends failed to obtain admission.

I managed to secure the recommendation of Mr Matthews, my primary school headmaster, so it was all down to the interview. I knew how much this meant to my parents: it was the first time anybody in the family had done anything like this. I was the oldest child, not only in our immediate family, but also out of all my cousins. And, as we were still relative newcomers to Liverpool, I had the feeling that it was not only the family's eyes which were on me, but also the wider community's. So, off we all nervously went one evening, my parents and I, to the interview, where, amongst other very general things, I was asked what my favourite subject was, and which was my least favourite. Although I later enjoyed studying languages, at that particular time I was having some issues with French, and quite cheerily told the interviewers that it was my least favourite subject. When they enquired why that was so, I just as cheerily told them that I thought the teacher was not very good. When they asked who the teacher was, I told them without hesitation, not appreciating at the time that she was the mother of two brothers at the Blue Coat. The interviewers smiled and said I should be more careful in what I say. Something of a *faux pas*, then – not that I would have known what that meant. Luckily for me, it was not deemed so great an offence that it prevented me from being offered a place and, in due course, I arrived, all smart and scared witless, for my first day. My father was thrilled and proud, and everyone else around me seemed quite impressed, too. Things seemed to be coming together after three years in our new surroundings.

I have great memories of my seven years at the Blue Coat. My academic achievements were modest – I did enough to progress and ultimately secure a place at university – but I met some of the funniest, sharpest guys one could have the good fortune to meet. And that included the teachers. My personal favourite was my Latin/history/religious studies teacher, Phil Watson. Not only was he a great teacher, but he had that finest of qualities in that role, namely, the ability to establish a great rapport with his pupils. I returned to the school in 2011 to speak at the Founders' Day Service and asked about Mr Watson. I was informed that although he was approaching retirement, he was still regarded as something of a legend at the school. I sadly missed out on meeting him on this occasion, but the visit brought back some great memories. One of which was that he once told us that for years the headmaster had called him Dave, and he did not dare correct him. The headmaster was Mr Peter Arnold-Craft – ex-Oxbridge, stern disciplinarian, well capable of putting the fear of God into any teacher, let alone 11-year-old newcomer to the school. Another memory I have of Mr Watson reflects some of the changes society has undergone in the last quarter of a century. In the Eighties, when it was still common for pupils to be caned or "slippered", the last thing one expected from one's teachers was much in the way of sensitivity. They were the teachers and, by and large, the pupils knew their place, especially at schools such as the Blue Coat. If you managed to strike up some friendly banter with a teacher then that was just a bonus. I remember in one of his lessons early on in my school life, Mr Watson made a couple of jokes about me and my race or religion. I thought nothing of it and laughed along. This was, after all, one of my favourite teachers. I was nevertheless surprised when, at the end of the lesson, he called me back and said words to the effect of, "Look, I say such things in jest, but I hate racism, and if ever you are offended by my comments, you only have to say so and I won't make them any more." I told him it was no problem for me. I am sure that over the years since I left school he will have adapted his rapport with the pupils to take into account the changes in what is expected of people in his position. But, to be perfectly honest, I think I much prefer his approach to the mealy-mouthed political correctness which prevails now, and which hides all manner of unsavoury views. Now, people who hold such views realise they cannot freely air them in public and that simply makes them more entrenched in their prejudices, blaming their victims as if political correctness was something invented by them.

The school was not only an enjoyable time for me, it helped shape my future in ways that I did not fully appreciate at the time. As I was one of only two Muslim pupils in my year, my friends were unsurprisingly all white English lads. But, culturally, although there was a big gap between my life at home and that at school, I did not feel alienated or marginalised in any way. I seemed to get by adequately enough with one foot in each culture, knowing that I was a Muslim, yet comfortable with my English friends, never feeling left out despite having to miss out on various "social events" as we grew up. This is something that does trouble many young Muslims, and may well impact on my own children's lives in due course. But, for me, it was never an issue. Growing up, I had no interest in going to parties, pubs or clubs and that, coupled with the knowledge that my parents would not allow it anyway, meant that the boundaries were clearly drawn and there was no chance of them being encroached upon. I had sufficient personality to make friendships, and did not feel my life was any the less enjoyable for its social limitations. The Eighties progressed enjoyably enough for me, and it looked as though I would succeed in getting the education I needed in order to attain my goals.

The main goal, which I had announced at the ripe old age of nine, was to become a barrister. Now, that sounds either mightily impressive or annoyingly precocious, depending on your approach to these things. But, if truth be told, it was probably neither. My parents, like every other Asian parent on the planet, had told everybody that I was going to become a doctor. To be fair, they did not just go round announcing it to all and sundry, but, if ever anybody enquired about what I wanted to be when I grew up, that was the answer my parents always gave. For a short while, I was happy to go along with this, until one day it dawned on me that, as I hated blood and goo, perhaps going into medicine was not the ideal career choice. I was also smart enough to have realised that a close family friend, who was a barrister, was earning good money, and was clearly somebody who had my father's respect. So, without knowing exactly what a barrister did, I started to proclaim that I wanted to be one. Once a month, the Muslim community would gather for the meeting of a Pakistani cultural organisation, the Circle of Literary Friends, who met to discuss Pakistani history and related Islamic topics. The events consisted of talks, food, and general socialising; it was a great way of getting to know other members of the not very large community. One of my father's good friends founded the group, and we children were not only roped into attending the meetings, but we were also made to speak at them. Even for a good teenager like me the meetings were utterly boring. But for my father, who saw the bigger picture, they were an opportunity for me to develop my public speaking. He would write a speech, sometimes in English, sometimes in Urdu (which certainly impressed the other families), and I would practise it at home before dutifully reading it out in front of everyone. I was pretty good at it – I even received a Young Speaker of the Year award, presented by David Alton MP (now Lord Alton) – but, when I was rehearsing, I just felt like I was being punished.

It was also an opportunity for my father to put to use his considerable knowledge about Pakistani and Muslim history. He was something of an authority on Jinnah, the founder of Pakistan, as well as on Iqbal, the poet and Islamic scholar who was the inspiration behind the movement for Muslim independence. At the time, all I did was read out what my father wrote, and very little of the knowledge actually permeated through my skull. But one thing that did get through was how much respect my father had for these two individuals. Both of these men had been called to the Bar in England. Jinnah went on to forge such a successful career in London that he had a chauffeur-driven Bentley in the 1930s! Iqbal, however, was more of a thinker – perhaps dreamer – who realised that the ill-treatment of Muslims in India would only be ended by the creation of a separate Muslim state. He was also, by all accounts, a wonderful poet who, through his verse, lamented the state of Muslims in the world and exhorted them to improve themselves so that they were befitting the vicegerency bestowed upon them by their Creator.

My secondary education, therefore, was all geared towards this one goal: gaining a place at a respectable university in order to obtain the law degree I would need to become a barrister. As so often in my life, I was incredibly lucky – or, as I would say, blessed. I had secured admission to the best school in Liverpool on the back of a recommendation from my headmaster and a mildly amusing interview. I had somehow managed to get 10 O levels – which sounded good, even though the grades were hardly spectacular. And now, I had managed to fail one of my A levels and still gain a place at Manchester University, one of the best universities in the country (especially for law), while harder working, brighter pupils had narrowly missed out on their universities of choice. Not for the first time, I had landed on my feet and felt very fortunate.

I have no doubt that one of the reasons I did not perform particularly well in my A levels is that I decided to do my revision in our front lounge. This was where my father kept all his books, most of which were about religion. Instead of studying for my A level Economics, which was shockingly dull, I preferred to read these religious books, and it was here that my first genuine religious convictions were formed. Up until then, I had been content to believe in Islam simply because I had been taught to, but now my "beliefs" were beginning to develop.

I encountered a world which suddenly seemed to place me on a much firmer footing. Although I had adjusted well to occupying two cultures, my religious knowledge was fairly limited, and certainly did not fill me with confidence. I also knew next to nothing about Pakistani history and its personalities. Now, though, my father's books were not only introducing me to these topics, but were igniting a real interest in me. The endless conversations he had with his friends began to make sense, and I started to appreciate both their content and – just as importantly – their tone. It was not lost on me that the common themes in these conversations, and in his books – Islam, education, integrity and responsibility – were things that did not occur in combination as often as they should. Indeed, these books reflected a world of Islam which even I could see was notable by its absence.

Iqbal was reminding his audience of the past glories of the Muslim world, from Cordoba to Samarkand, but painfully pointing out that what was left behind was merely a shell, both in terms of the character of the people, and their faith. He was urging the Muslims of his day to awaken from their slumber, but little seemed to have changed in the following hundred years or so. Yes, there was now independence from colonial rule for many Muslims throughout the world, but this, in itself, had not necessarily improved their lot, nor had it advanced the respect of the Muslim world. Jinnah had undoubtedly succeeded in gaining an independent Muslim state, but what had Pakistan achieved on the world stage since? It may well have suffered from his untimely death, as well as from being hamstrung by India and Britain at its inception, but how many of its faults could it really attribute to others? The rampant corruption, dishonesty and lack of human dignity – which, even as a teenager, I could see – were a world away from the integrity displayed by Jinnah. And to add insult to injury, instead of working to overcome these flaws, there were too many Pakistanis who were content to point out that Jinnah was a "bad" Muslim who drank alcohol, which was forbidden in Islam. This was to be my first understanding of the extent to which the form of Islam was beginning to overshadow the substance. But such thoughts were only just being sown.

Distracting though they were, I got the grades I needed, and so, in the summer of 1987, my father had the pre-university "chat" with me. He had never really had to tell me about the "do's and don'ts" of life, as I had generally been well behaved. As for the *facts* of life – well, there was no way he was going to explain them in any detail. Now, however, a conversation took take place which involved both the facts of life *and* some do's and don'ts. As ever, it was all conducted in a very British way, with tremendous dignity (aloofness) and respect (shyness), partly because he did not want to say much (and I certainly did not want to hear much). He said a few words about one's "character", and how university was the place where this would be tested. I, with my characteristic insight, understood this to mean, "no hanky-panky with your tickle tackle". And, there, matters were left to rest. I didn't find his approach particularly difficult, as I still saw life in stark terms: things were black or white, right or wrong, and if you followed the rules you would be fine.

Of course, I did not even set eyes on a woman until I got married some twenty odd years later. But, that inherent virtue aside, I was particularly ill-equipped for such endeavours. I had been to an all-boys school, I had not had any female friends, let alone any girlfriends, and here I was in a flat in Manchester with seven English lads who were hardly the last word in romantic acumen. A couple of them had girlfriends back home, one had the odd female "acquaintance" but, being from Yorkshire, generally preferred beer to women, and the rest were practically hand-picked by the good Lord Himself (moving as He does in mysterious ways) to ensure that I was not tempted to stray. What followed, therefore, were three years wasted – I mean, *spent* on getting a law degree, and not much else. Looking back on my university years, I am pretty sure that if I had befriended some Muslim lads, the chances of emerging with an unblemished "character" might not have been so great. Certainly, for many of them, it was the opportunity they had been waiting for: no parents, no restrictions – in fact, nothing to stop them enjoying themselves.

There was another type of Muslim student, of course. I would see them every week, in a makeshift prayer room, conducting the Friday prayer. They were undoubtedly sincere and devout, but, strangely, I was not particularly drawn to them. They seemed like decent guys, but they were hardly the kind of people I wanted to hang out with. There was also an Asian Society, predominantly made up of students with an Indian background, and they were much more fun-loving. But bhangra gigs were not really my thing, so I did not join their number. I ended up spending most of my time with my flatmates – a pretty decent bunch, who had no issues with me being Muslim and not joining in their nights out, and were actually good fun. We got on so well that, give or take one or two changes to the group, most of us stayed together for the full three years. They suited me: I had grown up with few Muslim friends, so it would have felt strange and artificial to go looking for some now.

The serious Muslim students seemed a bit too "Muslim" – which I was not used to – so I soon began to attend the local mosque in Manchester for the Friday prayer. This was a typical, Pakistani-run mosque where if you had forgotten to wear a cap some helpful soul would place one on your head, oblivious to the fact that this is not actually a religious requirement. The sermons were delivered by an imam who seemed to model himself on the Pharaoh rather than the Prophet, entering the mosque like a king entering his castle, and then proceeding to deliver a sermon of such fiery rhetoric that the simple masses listening were left awestruck, but utterly unenlightened. It was not that he was advocating violence or anything, just that he was all about the style rather than the substance, and rarely, if ever, did you leave the mosque thinking that you had learned something. To this day I find it depressing to think of the number of mosques up and down the country at which the opportunity to address, and thereby educate, a captive audience is squandered on a weekly basis.

What made it all the more frustrating was that in the late Eighties, as a result of the *Satanic Verses* affair, Muslims were thrust on to the front pages, and thus in need of articulate, intelligent leaders to speak up on our behalf – leaders who were suddenly conspicuous by their absence. Not only was there little in the way of impressive leadership, but the community had to suffer the indignity of being lectured to by the likes of Douglas Hurd MP about how it was expected to behave. The same community which had been regarded, for the twenty years it had been in Britain, as hard-working and law-abiding, never rioting and never complaining, was now portrayed as villainous. There may well have been a legitimate debate to be had about the limits of free speech, but Muslims were not invited to participate – certainly not as equals. They were simply told what was expected of them. Salman Rushdie was held aloft by the literary worthies for his amazing insight into the immigrant experience, but such an experience was more accurately, and amusingly, recalled by the average mini-cab driver in Blackburn. People like my father had come to this country and worked day and night not just to improve themselves, but also to make a contribution to their new home, while at the same time struggling to hold on to their religious values and identity. Yet it was Rushdie who was the hero. I found the whole episode bewildering and depressing, but it taught me some valuable lessons about leadership, education, and the portrayal of Islam by the Western media.

So university was not the greatest period of my life. And, to be fair, I should have made more of it than I did, at least on the gaining knowledge front. One highlight, however, was my friendship with Andrew Yerrakadu. Andrew was a student from New York whose parents were originally from Guyana, and of an Indian background, which meant he looked as Asian as me. We could have probably passed for brothers, although he was a talented weightlifter, so about twice my size. We got on great and spent most days together. He rarely drank and, as he had a girlfriend back in the USA, he was not one for chasing the ladies either. He was a practising Christian, and would have gone in to the ministry if he had not chosen law, but his explanation of various Christian beliefs was totally new to me. Here was a Christian who did not believe that the phrase "Son of God" was to be understood literally to refer to the physical offspring of the Creator. He had no issues with the theory of evolution, either, which to me seemed bizarre, as my own religious outlook was still one of absolutes, and only allowed room for what I had read in the books. Evolution did not form part of that. Put simply, he was both very religious and very thoughtful, and this was the first time I had met somebody who seemed to inhabit his religious world so comfortably. Although I may not have realised it at the time, Andrew, together with my flatmates, would influence the way I approach being a Muslim in Britain; he began to introduce a little more colour into a life which had perhaps been too monochrome thus far.

I was not exactly a typical student, or even a typical Muslim student – whatever that might be. I did not have the kind of "fun" normally associated with undergraduate life, which would not have been so bad if I had emerged with some spectacular academic success. But that was never going to happen. Firstly, I was never that bright, and, secondly, I was doing a law degree simply because I wanted to be a lawyer, not because I had any interest in the law itself. Very soon after I started working, I realised that so little of the degree was relevant to what I was doing that I may as well have done a subject I was interested in – say, history or politics – and then done a conversion course to get me through to the Bar finals. But, of course, I believe everything happens for a reason, and what may have seemed like a wasted three years actually brought me into contact with people whose outlook on life influenced me in a positive way. At the time, it may have been frustrating to argue with Andrew about, say, the *Satanic Verses* (Lord knows Andrew loved to argue), but I later came to appreciate the benefits of such conversations. Andrew and I graduated and went to Bar school together in London, before he returned home to sit the New York Bar exams and I began my search for a pupillage.

I had applied to, amongst others, a set of chambers in Liverpool, which had a good reputation for criminal and family work (I was interested in the former). In order to select from the prospective pupils, a few of them would come to a London hotel, spend a weekend there conducting interviews and invite any candidates who impressed them to spend a day or two in chambers so that others could get to meet them. My interview took place on a Saturday morning.

It was my first pupillage interview, and it seemed to go well enough. Thankfully, they asked no legal questions that I can remember, preferring to concentrate on the more pressing issue of whether I was a red or a blue. Once I had given them the correct answer (LFC of course), the interview proceeded in a relaxed and friendly way, and I went back to Manchester reasonably pleased. Later that same day, they rang, asking me to spend the following Tuesday and Wednesday with them in Liverpool. So I went home for a few days, spent a couple of them in chambers, and at the end of the second day I was offered a pupillage.

It was only when I returned to London and nonchalantly announced that I had been offered a pupillage in Liverpool that I understood the enormity of what had happened. My simple-minded view up until then had been that you got all your pupillage offers and then decided which one to pick. But when I began to hear stories of students decorating their bathrooms with rejection letters, it dawned on me how lucky I was. My classmates, who were a tad more realistic than I was, could not believe that I had secured an offer within five days of my first pupillage interview. Once again, things had fallen into place for me without much effort or stress on my part. All I had to do was to pass the Bar exams, which I somehow managed the following summer. I could not begin to explain how this happened: 1990–1991 was the first year of the new Bar Vocational course and nobody had a clue what they were doing, tutors included. It all seemed like a lottery. Happily for me, my number came up and a new chapter of my life began.

In the autumn of 1991, I began my pupillage in what was then the chambers of David Harris QC. Robert, my pupil master, was great. To this day he remarks that he only ever asked me to do one piece of work in the whole of my pupil-lage, which he is still waiting for. I suppose it was his own fault for being so relaxed about things, and preferring to talk about his exotic holidays than anything particularly useful to me as a pupil. I do, however, recall one conversation with him that was not so relaxed. At the end of this particular day, when we had returned to chambers from court, he said he needed to speak to me. In fact, it was worse than that: he said, "David has asked me to speak to you." I was beside myself – what on earth could I had done so wrong that it prompted my head of chambers to speak to my pupil master? I sat down across the room from Robert. He seemed very nervous, which was not like him, so I figured things must be bad. He began with, "Well, what it is... I am not married... I live with a friend..." The penny dropped, but that did not stop Robert continuing the uncomfortable conversation. Or, at least, he tried to continue the conversation but, in the middle of our mutual discomfort, a shelf stacked with heavy law books came crashing to the ground. I could not help thinking, "Well, if that isn't Divine intervention, mate, I don't know what is!"

Joking aside, the allocation of my pupil master was another example of how things always worked out for me. I had no choice in Robert being my pupil master, but I am so lucky to have received the benefit of his experience and expertise, without his having to burden me with lots of work. I guess he thought that the profession would be demanding enough, and that all he had to do for the time being was to provide a little guidance, and a lot of good company. He certainly did that, and continued to share his time generously, long after my pupillage had ended. Other colleagues starting out in chambers had very demanding pupil masters, yet I was able to enjoy leisurely lunches and great conversation, whilst all the while learning how to do the job properly. Being Robert's pupil was such a joy that now, as his retirement approaches, it is worth noting the affection and indebtedness I feel towards him.

The rest of that decade involved little more than establishing myself in my career, buying a house in a decent part of town close to my parents, enjoying having money in my pocket and nice cars to drive, and nothing in the way of serious responsibility – at least, not outside of work hours. There was undoubtedly a change in the way I was being treated by people; it really did seem to make a difference when they discovered that I was a barrister. My father's friends gained a new degree of respect for me, and were more inclined to involve me in their conversations. These conversations were still along the same lines as when I was younger – their criticisms of religious leaders were no different – but I actually understood them now. I began to appreciate more of the nuance that they saw in their faith, but which had passed me by up until then. The fact that they managed to inject humour into these conversations also played a part in the development of my religious outlook: I began to realise that there was nothing in the Quran forbidding having a laugh.

In fact, I realised, there was much less forbidding in the Quran than many Muslims would have us believe. The more I read it, and other books about Islam, the more I realised that there was more to this faith than rules and regulations. For the time being, however, I did not have to concern myself unduly with such considerations. That was my father's department. He did the reading, thinking and discussing. I was free to concentrate on my career.

All that would change in 1999. My father had suffered from prostate cancer for several years and, although his initial treatment appeared to have been successful, by late 1998 the cancer had returned. When he retired from teaching in November 1998, one of the first things he wanted to get sorted was the operation to remove the prostate gland. He was booked in for his operation on the 19th March 1999. We were warned it would be a lengthy procedure, and that it would be somewhat complicated by the fact that he had previously undergone radiotherapy. It went well, though, and afterwards he was to spend a week or so recuperating in hospital. I took a few days off work to spend time with him, but he did not see the point of me sitting there all day.

On the 23rd March, I was planning to go in and see him in the afternoon. I was at home at about eleven o'clock in the morning when my sister rang to say the hospital had called urgently, telling us to get to there as soon as we could: my father had collapsed. I made my way from my house, and my sister took my mother. We arrived at the hospital at the same time, worried but not for a moment expecting the news we were about to receive. We were taken into a separate room, where we were told that my father had apparently had a heart attack, due to a pulmonary embolism, and had passed away. Our world had suddenly fallen apart.

My mother was beside herself. To this day, she understandably feels bitter that they were unable to enjoy his retirement. But that day in the hospital she felt like she had lost a limb. My father's best friend arrived a few minutes later, and could not believe the news he was hearing. I almost felt more sorry for him than myself, knowing that he and my father, who saw each other pretty much every day, had been looking forward to his retirement, when they could spend even more time together. Although my sisters and I were all grown up and involved in our careers by now, it began to dawn on us in the ensuing days just how much we had come to rely on my father, and how much of a void his passing would leave. He was the source of our family's respect, the voice of reason, the man to whom everyone turned for the answer. That was all gone now, and we would have to fend for ourselves. We obviously coped, but even now I look back on the three following years as a blur, in which I seemed to be operating on some kind of autopilot.

At the time, my father's death seemed like a big mistake. It was so unexpected that it just did not make sense. He had his retirement to look forward to, and so much still to offer, not just to us but to everyone he encountered. I, for one, had much still to learn from him. It took a long time for me to realise that, untimely though it may have been, it was part of a bigger plan.

A few months later, I was asked by some of his friends to attend a local inter-faith meeting so that his colleagues there could pass on their condolences to me in person. I did attend, met some wonderful people, appreciated the efforts they were making, and felt that perhaps I should carry on where my father had left off. I began to get involved in inter-faith work, and speak about Islam whenever opportunities presented themselves. Those opportunities in turn blossomed, and I found myself embarking on the path which would ultimately lead to this book.

3

Religion or science (or both)?

As a child, I dutifully obeyed both the requirements of my faith and my parents. Although they expected certain standards of behaviour from me, it was rare that they actually articulated any specific demands. Much was left unsaid with regard to what my sisters and I should or should not do. My mother's own recollection from her childhood, that her parents only had to look at her in order for her to check her behaviour, may well be something of an exaggeration, but, speaking as a parent myself now, I can confirm that unquestioning obedience from one's offspring is not as prevalent today as it was when I was younger. My parents simply did not need to spell things out to me: I knew what was expected. And, although they had been relatively liberal in the way they introduced me to our religion, it was not open for debate that I was going to be a practising Muslim. Even so, no amount of good parental teaching can replace having one's own conviction about something, so although my father's conversations, both with me and with others, were a positive influence on my outlook, they were just a small – albeit welcome – step on my own journey. I was fortunate enough to have access to his books, and it was this that helped me establish a firm foothold in Islam by way of personal conviction rather than upbringing.

Many of my friends took a different route to confirming their faith. Some were content to do as they were taught by their parents, and did not feel the need to explore their beliefs. They dutifully abided by most of the requirements and, as long as they were seen to be practising Muslims, all was well. Others were more thoughtful and willing to look a little deeper. Often, they were unable to discuss their thoughts with their families and sought out the company of those with a similar outlook. As we shall see later, such closed groups had their own problems. Not all would go on to become the radicalised youngsters we read of in Ed Husain's *The Islamist*, but most wanted to mutually confirm the unquestionable rightness of all aspects of orthodox faith.

There had been student Islamic societies since the 1970s, but they got a shot in the arm after 1979. The fall of the Shah in Iran, and the invasion of Afghanistan by the Russians, put Muslims back into the headlines, and this coincided with the second generation of Muslims in the UK being in full-time education. Islamic student societies were good for all concerned. Youngsters could now be outside the confines of their homes legitimately, and parents could rest seemingly assured that their children were socialising with other Muslims, thereby protecting them from the ills of Western temptation. (This was not necessarily always true. In the late Eighties there was a Muslim youth camp held in Hull over a period of several days that I could have attended. But I had no inclination to go and stay with the "brothers", knowing that for many of them it was just an excuse to get away from their strict homes for a few days and let their hair down. The joy that came with being flicked by a wet towel was lost on me.)

My suspicions proved well founded after the camp dispersed when it was disclosed that three boys from Liverpool had been expelled late one night. They had apparently been caught going into Hull town centre to meet up with some similarly errant "sisters". Despite their protestations about only being after a pizza ("Pizza what?" they were asked) they were told to leave the camp immediately. Fortunately for them, they had a car. Unfortunately for them, they had fathers who would have beaten them soundly had they returned home in disgrace, so they decided instead to head off to a friend's house in Kent. The last (disclosable) part of the story involves a policeman knocking on the driver's door window at about four in the morning and waking him to inform him that the hard shoulder on the M6 was not intended for the lads to get their heads down for a while. To this day, I hear Muslims from around the country recall the Hull camp circa 1987, and the Liverpool lads who were expelled, and I am proud to inform them that those guys are now three of my closest friends.

Happily, I did not have to rely on such camps, nor indeed on any of my peers, to develop my interest in Islam. I had read enough by the time I went to university to feel confident in my beliefs, and they were yet to be challenged in any meaningful way. Inevitably, once there, I began to realise that, for some people, especially many who regarded themselves as intelligent and rational, religious people were to be pitied for their affliction, at best to be humoured: their belief in a supernatural being was comparable to a child's belief in Father Christmas, and reflected a need in primitive minds to explain away the vagaries of life. With the arrival of scientific enlightenment, religion had surely been superseded, and those who clung to it were flying in the face of all reason. This attitude undoubtedly had an effect on me. At times, I was riled by its proponents, although the predominant feeling I had was a desire to learn how to counter such accusations. I was "religious", but did not regard myself as inferior to, or any less rational than, the next man. As for the scientific side of things, I was hardly well placed to address such arguments, seeing as one of my claims to fame was that I had emerged from a top school with 10 O levels, none of which was for a science subject.

Despite my lack of interest in – and worthwhile knowledge of – scientific matters, I did happen to read a book called *The Bible, the Qu'ran and Science* by a French doctor called Maurice Bucaille. It turned out to be one of those life-changing books that one rarely encounters, the first step on a journey of reconciliation between my religious beliefs and science and reason. In essence, Bucaille's conclusion was that there was nothing in the Quran that was contrary to scientific fact. That itself did not particularly surprise me, but more impressive than the conclusion itself was the way in which Bucaille approached his task. He rightly assessed that the Quran made observations on matters ordinarily regarded as belonging to the realm of scientific enquiry, and therefore needed to be considered further to see whether what was said therein was consistent with modern scientific findings. Impressively, Bucaille determined that he would have to learn Arabic in order to consider those verses properly. He did so, and, after his subsequent investigations, concluded that the Quran simply could not have been composed by a mere mortal. I was staggered, and somewhat ashamed, to learn that this man's spirit of enquiry had led to him learning a language alien to him simply to enhance his knowledge. I, being a practising Muslim, had contented myself then, as now, with relying on translations of my own Holy Book.

Reconciling religion and science was not a straightforward task, for a number of reasons. For a start, I was never particularly academic. I had developed a pragmatic approach to learning which enabled me to get to the next stage of whatever it was that I was involved in, but little further. It also did not help that, at the time, I was not very interested in science. The exercise, therefore, was conducted in fits and starts, and I did not give it high priority; I was much more engaged by the mundane concerns of Muslims. I also found it troubling that many of the accusations levelled at religion did seem to have some support. I was painfully aware that most of the Muslims I encountered, particularly the older generation, were not only little versed in matters of science, but also insisted on retaining views which were irrational and superstitious in the extreme. To me, it was not groundbreaking to think that there was a Divine Architect behind the universe; many people, much cleverer than myself, shared that view. But it did not follow that they should then accept as truth every last assertion made in a "religious" text. Yet that is precisely what many religious people I knew actually did. It was as if, to them, following a faith meant discarding reason completely. They were content to accept unquestioningly the many myths that often accompanied religion, and did not stop to consider the possibility that such myths were simply a way of conveying a particular message to a particular community at a particular time, and did not, in themselves, constitute some kind of eternal truth. Perhaps more importantly from a Muslim point of view, such people did not even heed the Quran, which exhorts its readers to exercise the power of reason their Maker has granted to them.

It is perhaps surprising that religious belief still prevails. Despite the many flaws of its adherents, the idea of religion itself has not only not disappeared, but is actually in the midst of a resurgence. The fact is that most of humanity, in most of the world, throughout most of history, has held what can only be described as some kind of religious belief. It has encountered formidable adversaries, not least the onslaught of scientific enquiry, but it has never been extinguished. It has had to respond to the attacks, and at times be deeply self-critical, but still some of the most intellectual, "scientific" people around have deeply held religious beliefs. Religion has, undoubtedly, had to evolve. But the fact that it differs in some respects to its former incarnations does not, of itself, prove it is untrue.

And nor, for that matter, does stating that religion satisfies a human need prove that God does not exist. It is perhaps here that we need to draw the most important distinction. It is surely the existence, or otherwise, of God, that the argument should be about, rather than which of the disparate and diverse beliefs of those who purport to be his devotees is the "correct" one. There are those who suggest that human beings are "hard-wired" to be religious, and it may be that there is some truth in this, particularly as many religious people, Muslims included, believe that humans possess something of the Divine Spirit. Whatever we may choose to call this, whether it is the soul, or the conscience, there is something that seems to distinguish us from the rest of the universe, despite the fact that at a molecular level we are all the same.

The resurgence of religious belief is not necessarily a good thing, nor the best argument in its favour. It cannot be denied that it has, at times, operated as an opiate, dulling the senses of the masses and encouraging them to behave in irrational and destructive ways. Equally, it has, on occasion, proved to be an obstacle to freedom and democracy. And it has undoubtedly been used as a tool of power. Yet these very same criticisms can, and do, apply to other systems of thought, and ways of life, whether they involve a deity or not. It is understandable that the likes of Richard Dawkins and Christopher Hitchens should highlight the crimes of those who profess a belief in God, and yet atheists have committed just as many crimes, and it is hardly rational to denounce the former but not the latter. It does not follow as a matter of logic, or of practice, that discarding God automatically leads to freedom, happiness and an elevation of thought. The same human flaws which operate to the detriment of religious people also exist in those without religious faith, and result in similar problems. The goal, therefore, should be the eradication of those flaws; it is not enough to suggest that they only exist because of a particular belief system. Hatred, greed, intellectual laziness, envy and mean-spiritedness are not the sole preserve of believers.

Just as it is right to acknowledge that religious belief has been detrimental to individuals and societies, it should also be recalled that it has uplifted and inspired many others.

There are those who can only recall the negative impact of Roman Catholic belief, for example, and forget how much positive impact it has had on the arts in the Western world. Religion has not just influenced major thinkers and leaders who have contributed to the world, it has also inspired communities to fight against injustice and oppression. The belief in a cause greater than oneself can lead to difficulties, but it can also provide the impetus to challenge an oppressive status quo. There was a time when Islam freed the enslaved, empowered women, gave life to the female infant who was condemned to death, and provided equality and dignity to the downtrodden. The fact that it may not be fulfilling such noble purposes now should give cause for reflection, but not for jettisoning the entire premise of religion. Although it is not always allowed to flourish, the noble potential of religion is, in my view, one reason why it cannot and will not fade into obscurity.

To some, the challenges science poses for religion simply cannot be overcome. Religion, they maintain, involves vague assertions about matters which cannot be established empirically and, in some cases, can be positively shown to be false. Evolution is the trump card played by those who wish to "prove" the false nature of religious faith. The "Creation myth", they say, is simply that: a myth which holds that the universe was created in six days, rather than the billions of years we now know to be the case. Two random people called Adam and Eve were not mysteriously dropped on to the planet to propagate and set forth the chain of events that led to us. Accordingly, there is no paradise of milk/honey/virgins waiting for us if we believe in the right god, or a hell of fire, eternal damnation and, presumably, girls who are not virgins, if we do not. Humanity has advanced to the extent that it understands all events to have a rational, scientific explanation; the idea of an "act of God", which was merely an explanation for the primitive, unsophisticated mind, exists now simply to help insurance companies avoid paying out on their policies. Not only does such an analysis take for granted that religious texts can only be understood literally, but it is also based on the premise that there are a finite number of questions to be asked about all that is in existence, and that scientific enquiry provides all the answers to these questions. Now, I have considered all this scientific stuff (albeit in an analysis which makes beginner's guides appear encyclopaedic) and come to this conclusion. After centuries of scientific enquiry, and billions of pounds spent on research and space travel, we are still not even close to knowing the extent of what is "out there". That is unsurprising, given the size of the universe. Perhaps more perplexing, however, is that we still do not have definitive answers about even the smallest units of matter. There are those who will not be moved from the conclusion that none of this proves the existence of God – and, of course, it does not, at least not in any empirical way. But others hold an opposing view, and conclude that not only does such scientific enquiry leave open the *possibility* of there being a God, but that actually the more one explores science, the more the idea of God as the answer becomes the only *rational* explanation. There are intellectual heavyweights who occupy both camps, so how does the layperson resolve the issue? Does it ultimately come down to a matter of faith? Faith in science or faith in religion? Are the two incompatible? When we talk about faith are we talking about blind faith?

Or is there such a thing as a rational, evidence-based faith?

It was the numbers that convinced me. If we take as our definition of rational, "that which is consistent with or based upon reason", then we understand that exercising one's rational capacity means engaging one's mind rather than one's emotions. (And, of course, we only use a tiny fraction of our brains' potential at any given time. It remains a mystery what amazing feats we could achieve if we tapped into our full potential. There are people who suffer from conditions such as autism who have phenomenal mathematical capabilities, despite not having had any formal training in that field. And it has been suggested that tapping into the reserves of the brain's immense power could free up other hidden talents, such as telepathy and extra-sensory perception. Whether there is anything in such suggestions is beyond the remit of this discussion but, if there is, it would have significant implications for the whole idea of religion.) When exercising our powers of reason, however, we find that there are instances where a given proposition, which began as reasonable, can become unreasonable. The proposition may well be theoretically possible, in terms of pure logic, but so improbable that it is not practically possible.

The scale of what is "out there" matters to me for two reasons. Firstly, it has implications for my analysis of what is reasonable or rational. When numbers are beyond comprehension, it can be hard to accept that they occurred by chance. As we have noted, my lack of scientific background may well explain my readiness to be amazed by the numbers I encountered, but this only provides a partial explanation. The facts are staggering for anyone.

It was a complete shock for me to discover that the solar

system did not accord to the straightforward picture that I had in my mind, the one I had learned at school, which had the sun at one side of the page, Pluto at the furthest point across from it, and our planet, Earth, occupying a spot in between the two. I struggled to get my head around even the initial facts I was discovering. For example, I hadn't known that all the planets, moons, asteroids and other bits and pieces of the solar system occupy less than one-trillionth of the available space! I hadn't realised that the pictures I had seen had to put everything close together just to make it all visible on a single page. And that there is not just a lot of space *between* the planets but a lot of space *beyond* them. So Pluto, rather than marking the end of the solar system, is, in fact, only one 50-thousandth of the way to the edge of it. The crazy numbers were beginning to multiply.

The solar system, however huge it is, does not signify all that is out there. It is just one member of a vast galaxy, the Milky Way, containing perhaps 200 to 400 *billion* stars, of which the sun is just one. This galaxy is roughly 100,000 light years in diameter (a light year being 5,878,000,000,000 miles) – so big that even if we were able to travel across it at the speed of light it would take us hundreds of generations to reach the other side. Having established that the Milky Way is unimaginably huge, I next learned that it is, in fact, only one galaxy among some 100 to 200 billion – some scientists even estimate 500 billion. And each galaxy contains billions of stars. One estimate, therefore, of the number of planets in the universe is ten billion trillion. At least that has cleared that up, then! If only. It may help us begin to appreciate the extent of the universe (about a million million million million or 1,000,000,000,000,000,000,000,000 miles across), but that is only the *visible* universe. There are theories that the universe at large, or meta-universe, is much larger still, and that the number of light years to the edge of this unseen universe would be written not "with ten zeros, not even a hundred, but with millions".

Which brings me to the second reason that the scale of all that is out there was important to me. It put some perspective, however surreal, on my presuming to question why, if there was a Creator, I could not perceive him. "I" could not even be described as a speck on a dot on a speck on a dot, so how was I qualified to question the existence of the Creator of all that existed out there, particularly as I had not even learned to use anywhere near the full potential of my brain? It must be said that just because the universe, or even meta-universe, is so vast, it does not necessarily follow that there has to be a Creator. It may just be that it is part of human nature to be impressed by magnitude.

And after all, the very size of the universe means that, "If there are many universes, each governed by a differing set of numbers, there will be one where there is a particular set of numbers suitable to life. We are in that one." So the sheer scale of it all means that there is bound to be some place where life could form, and, happily for us, we happen to be in that place.

For me, however, this was an insufficient explanation. Firstly, because it relied too much upon chance, and secondly, because, given its size, the human mind is bound to struggle to comprehend the extent of the universe – what is more surprising, is the fact that it also seems to struggle with even the smallest units of existence.

On my scientific quest, I discovered that living organisms

are made up of cells, which in turn are made up of billions of molecules of many hundreds of different types. The average human cell is 20 microns wide, or about two-hundredths of a millimetre, and it is in this tiny area that we find the variety of molecules, such as the billion ATP molecules, and the minimum of 100 million protein molecules. This, of course, is not as small as it gets. Molecules consist of at least two atoms. Each atom is one ten-millionth of a millimetre. Small enough? Unfortunately not. In the 19th century it was a sufficient explanation to say that matter consisted of atoms, but within a hundred years it was discovered that atoms themselves have their constituent parts: protons, which have a positive electrical charge, electrons, which have a nega-tive electrical charge, and neutrons which have no charge. Neutrons and protons make up the atom's nucleus, itself one-millionth of a billionth of the full volume of the atom, but containing almost all the atom's mass. We still have not identified the smallest unit within the atom. Quarks and gluons form protons and neutrons, while neutrinos possess one ten-millionth of the mass of an electron...

The facts about the size of the constituent parts of the atom are perplexing enough on their own, without us even considering the behaviour of those constituent parts. When we do, we discover a sub-atomic world where electrons can jump from one orbit to another without travelling across any intervening space, a world of quantum physics which requires two bodies of laws, quantum and gravitational, to explain what is going on. It was in order to (attempt to) draw the two together that superstring theory (and its eleven dimensions) was formulated. So much for my ten O levels!

We have seen how perplexing the world of big numbers

is; further study shows how the micro-world is no easier to fathom. Some of the numbers we have encountered thus far are so huge (estimates of between 100 and 200 billion galaxies for example, or the 23 trillion molecules in a human cell), that it is easy to think that all this science is very imprecise. Yet there are other numbers which suggest it is anything but. One example is the precise calculation of the way in which hydrogen transforms into helium by converting seven one-thousandths of its mass to energy. If that value is lowered slightly, say from 0.07 to 0.06 per cent, then the transformation could not take place, and the universe would consist of hydrogen and nothing else. Similarly, if the value were raised to 0.08 per cent the conditions that we need for our survival simply would not exist. The question is: what is maintaining this very fine balance? Is it just by pure chance that the whole enterprise is kept afloat?

The unlikelihood of chance playing any significant role in the origin of life is illustrated by the process of protein formation. For the process to work, a number of amino acids need to assemble in a particular order. In order, for example, to make collagen (a common protein), 1,055 amino acids need to be assembled in exactly the right sequence... spontaneously and autonomously! (Even for a less complex protein, its production by random events is practically impossible, never mind for the hundreds of thousands of proteins which we actually rely upon.) And once the amino acids are in the right sequence, the protein must then fold itself into a very specific shape. And, having achieved that, the protein needs to reproduce, which it cannot do without DNA – which begs the question how proteins and DNA first came into existence. How is it that such ordered and complex self-assembly can take place?

There have been famous experiments, such as that of Stanley Miller in 1953, which have attempted to synthesise life. Not only have they been unsuccessful (save for some "inorganic" molecules), but they have been unsuccessful in controlled conditions. When life was first created on Earth, however, it did not occur in laboratory conditions. There would have been a myriad of hostile environmental forces that the initial cell would have had to contend with. Assuming for a moment that life did spontaneously spark into existence, and avoided being destroyed by the next gust of wind, crack of lightning or drop of rain, then, having achieved that improbable success, it would have had to replicate that initial "coincidence" many times over, in adverse conditions, in order to even begin to achieve the kind of complexity that could precede life as we know it. Could this really be achieved by chance, or was there a master programmer involved? Which of the two explanations is the reasonable one? When we consider, for example, the simple amoeba, which consists of one cell but carries 400,000,000 pieces of information in its DNA, the idea of a master programmer does not seem so far-fetched.

It is perhaps in the genetic field that the notion of a programmer is most apt. Living cells appear to consist of a veritable Aladdin's cave of information. Inside the nucleus of the human cell are the chromosomes that contain all the information and instructions required to create and maintain us. They are made up of DNA, almost two metres of it in each microscopic cell, and possibly as much as 20 billion kilometres of it inside our bodies. Each piece of DNA contains some 3.2 billion letters of coding. There is, therefore, an inordinate number of unique possible combinations that make us what we are. One estimate for the number of possible combinations is a one, followed by more than three billion zeros! Did all this information come into our cells by chance or was it programmed into them by an outside force, or God? The idea of it happening by chance is unfeasible to me – all the more so when I am reminded that, "All the tiny, deft chemical processes that animate cells – the cooperative efforts of nucleotides, the transcription of DNA into RNA – evolved just once and have stayed pretty well fixed ever since, across the whole of nature." This, no doubt, partly explains why scientists themselves still use phrases such as the "mystery of life" or "miracle of life"; the more we think we are approaching certainty and finality in our findings, the more questions we seem to unearth.

As Bill Bryson has said: "The upshot of all this is that we live in a universe whose age we can't quite compute, surrounded by stars whose distance from us and each other we don't altogether know, filled with matter we can't identify, operating in conformance with physical laws whose properties we don't truly understand."

At this point, it is perhaps worth pausing to ask what exactly we mean by proof. As a barrister, I often use scientific evidence. This could be, for example, fingerprint or DNA evidence said to link the defendant to the crime. When presenting such evidence to the jury, the scientific expert in question will often assert that the chances of the fingerprint belonging to anyone other than the defendant are, for example, in the order of 1 in 50 million. Such a statistical probability essentially means, so the prosecution would say, that as far as the jury is concerned, this is proof *beyond reasonable doubt*.

Given some of the statistical probability I was encountering in the precise realm of science, what conclusions would it be reasonable or rational for me to draw? It is considered entirely reasonable to decide the fate of a man on the basis of the above statistical probability figures. Yet, when we consider the probability of various components in the universe coming into being by chance (let alone the probability of everything coming together to make the whole enterprise work), we seem ready to accept random chance as the explanation. Is it reasonable or rational, in such circumstances, to believe in a Divine creator who is beyond the limited comprehension of human beings? Or can it properly be concluded that such figures show that random chance is behind the origins and workings of the universe?

So where does this all leave us? I do not by any stretch mean to trivialise the importance of scientific enquiry. The fact remains that our powers of reason are our best hope in navigating our way through life, at least with some measure of understanding. However, understanding the world around us does not necessarily provide all the meaning we need in order to live out our full potential. We can figure out how the world works and, with this knowledge, attempt to harness the forces of nature so we can exploit them and master the physical world. But we need to remember two things.

Firstly, there is more to life than the physical world: we are composed of the same molecules as all the inanimate things around us, yet we possess a consciousness which science has thus far been unable to explain. Secondly, if we are going to harness nature, we should not do so in the absence of a system of values; scientific endeavour does not operate in a vacuum. It is worth considering, for example, that the vast majority of scientific research and development expenditure goes on military programmes. Clearly, this is the result of decisions taken in certain quarters, decisions which invariably involve value judgements. It is as a result of such value judgements that decisions are made to fund the development of ever more sophisticated weaponry rather than the search for a cure for cancer. The pure exercise of reason does not necessarily assist us in making the right decisions and may, in fact, lead us further down a destructive path – destructive to our environment or to our humanity. The values upon which we act, therefore, will not be found in science books.

For Muslims, these values are found primarily in their Holy Book, the Quran. Not only does the Quran purport to contain the guidance that humanity requires to live a materially and spiritually enriched life, but it also provides the "evidence" which enables us to move from a passive agnostic belief to an active belief in God. It is a book that exhorts the reader to investigate the natural world in order to arrive at a reasoned belief, rather than relying on blind faith. It is a book that time and again addresses itself to people "of understanding". Nowhere does it hand over authority to a class of so-called "religious scholars" or "mullahs" to lord it over the masses. On the contrary, the word *ulema* (plural of *alim*, meaning scholar) is used in the Quran to refer to those who are urged to ponder the rain cycle, animal life, plant life and other aspects of nature. It refers to zoologists, botanists, meteorologists – in short, it refers to scientists.

During the Golden Age of Muslim civilisation, a time

of intellectual and artistic achievement, the great mathematicians, physicians, poets and artists, were also religious scholars. Knowledge was not defined narrowly to mean just religious knowledge but, rather, it meant a spirit of enquiry encouraged by the Quran. It is a sad indictment of the state of many contemporary Muslim societies that the word *ulema* is understood simply to refer to the bearded guys, armed with a smattering of religious rulings, who are entitled to make pronouncements about how the faithful should live their lives.

The Quran urges humanity to fulfil its potential by understanding the world around it. The achievements of Muslim scientists in the Golden Age – which we shall look at in greater detail in due course – were not despite the Quran, but *because* of it. Not only did it contain the inspiration for scientific enquiry, but it also contained scientific references which could not have been authored by a human being in 7th-century Arabia. The findings of Maurice Bucaille, and others, seem to me to give some force to the notion that the Quran was not a human product but a divine work, nothing short of a miracle. After all, the Prophet Muhammad is the only possible author of this book, yet there is no suggestion that he ever authored any other document, let alone a world-changing mixture of prose and poetry. A Christian Arab friend, from my university days, once told me that he read the Quran not because he believed it, but because the Arabic was so perfect. It is a grand work of literature as much as anything else. According to Muslim history, the Holy Prophet was illiterate, yet here is a book the recitation of which reduced men to tears.

It is also a book which contains scientific material that

the Prophet would simply have been unaware of. There is a reference, for example, to two bodies of water (fresh and sea water) which do not mix. There is the fact that it uses two different Arabic words for "light" to refer to the sun and moon, one of which denotes something which generates its own light, the other of which refers to something with reflected light. Or the fact that the verses pertaining to embryology refer to the foetus as something which "clings": it was only discovered centuries later that the foetus does, indeed, cling to the uterus wall. These, and other examples, were sufficient to convince me that this was not a book authored by a human being.

Perhaps its greatest achievement is its assertion that this time it would be God Himself who would safeguard the book. Earlier scriptures may well have been revised and altered, but this was a message for eternity and would be protected. I could not understand how this promise had been kept, and that there were no subsequent "editions" of the Quran, unless it truly was safeguarded. I had not even done a fraction of the research that true scholars such as Bucaille could claim, but the little I had done was more than enough to convince me that here was the evidence for the existence of God.

Ultimately, then, my limited scientific enquiry does not move me further away from a belief in God, but, on the contrary, reinforces my understanding that there must be an intelligent force behind creation. It helps me make sense of what is around me, and, in developing even a rudimentary understanding of the complexity of life, I can begin to appreciate the wonders of the universe, and consider for myself what conclusions it is reasonable to draw from the available evidence. Science helped to rationalise my religious beliefs so that I did not satisfy myself with childish ideas of an old man with a white beard watching everything from the sky above, while at the same time appreciating that the creator of all that exists would inevitably be beyond human comprehension.

It also helped me begin to discard mythologies which may have served a particular purpose at a particular time, and focus instead on the values and principles underlying those mythologies, which should underpin the way I live my life. Science reinforces the Islamic view that there is an underlying unity in life and that we should not, therefore, compartmentalise the spiritual and material aspects but, rather, strive to understand the totality of our environment, thereby moving closer to our Creator. Only then are we best placed to benefit from the guidance available to us, and which we need in order to fulfil our potential and live a life befitting human beings, rather than other sentient creatures inhabiting the planet.

4

Have Muslims always been "thick"?

For centuries, Western civilisation has prevailed. It may be that in certain quarters there is a degree of anxiety about the future, a fear that the East will one day exert its not inconsiderable might – particularly given the apparently unlimited ambition and economic growth of the likes of China and India – but the fact remains, for the time being, that the West is regarded as the rightful home of the leaders of the world. This belief has become so ingrained that, in the West at least, we even see our current economic plight as a temporary aberration, rather than the result of an underlying structural or ideological weakness. Whether our views on the economic situation are accurate or not only time will tell, and we shall consider this further later on. For our present purposes, however, we will assume that the West has every right to feel pre-eminent, given its record of success, particularly in the field of scientific achievement and consequential material development.

There is no doubt that, particularly in the last six centuries, great leaps forward have been made in the West. But one also has to bear in mind that history is written by the victors. We all read Shakespeare at school, as any student of English should, but we would struggle to name any poets from other countries, which perhaps makes our belief that he is the greatest poet who ever lived less than robust. Our understanding of the rest of the world's contribution in other fields has similar limitations. It could be argued that an Anglophile or Eurocentric approach to such issues can hardly be criticised given where we live, but, in the age of the global village, a bit of insight into the thinking of others would not go amiss. Nowadays, it makes sense, for business reasons, to have some respect for the sensibilities of the Chinese, and a similar outlook has informed the way we have dealt with oil rich Arab regimes in the past. Such "respect", however, is far removed from genuine understanding, and it is the latter that actually brings communities together, rather than allowing us simply to put up with each other.

We hear that our society is broken, yet we continue to ignore possible avenues towards a mutual understanding that could form the mortar to help us rebuild. Areas in which communities have traditionally been able to intermingle are becoming scarcer by the day; many old workplaces, such as factories and mills, have disappeared, and even the nature of the high street is altering considerably, with an increase in online shopping and out of town retail parks. Extra thought, therefore, needs to be given to what can bring people together. The alternative is that our paths will diverge until it is too late to refer to where we live as a society. This is already happening in many English towns, and, sadly, ones with large Muslim communities. We need to address this sooner rather than later if we do not want the social cracks to widen. Muslims themselves need to wake up and ask whether they are contributing to an increased understanding or increased mistrust in their communities.

As a matter of urgency, we need to identify areas for mutual cooperation. Sometimes such cooperation can happen organically – there are practical projects, for example, that bring neighbourhoods together. Despite all the media coverage which suggests that Jews and Muslims are forever foresworn to despise each other, there are many Muslims actively seeking education for their children in Jewish schools – such as the King David Schools in Liverpool and Birmingham – because education is their priority. These schools, in turn, are happy to take Muslim pupils. Both communities benefit; it is a small step towards each other rather than in opposite directions. In 2012, at least one happy Jewish-Muslim story did find its way on to the BBC website: a synagogue in the USA opened its doors to the local Muslim community who needed some extra prayer space for the festival of Eid. Our shared humanity demands such effort, but we should not wait for practical needs to arise. There is a long history of intellectual cooperation which needs to be revived, and topics for discussion resuscitated.

One area of potential understanding which has been particularly neglected is that of Muslim scientific achievement. Not only did these achievements have a significant impact on the Western understanding of science, but they also often took place in Europe itself, and thus were European achievements just as much as they were Islamic ones. One of my favourite subjects at school was history, which I studied through to A level. Yet I do not recall at any stage being taught the history of Cordoba in Spain. Cordoba should be held up as a shining example of the benefits of cooperation: this was a city which, a thousand years ago, was described as the "ornament of the world", boasted facilities that the rest of Europe could only dream of, and achieved all this through the mutual endeavour and cooperation of the three monotheistic faith communities. Yet this story is deemed unworthy of telling to contemporary generations.

One might have thought that reminding ourselves of a time when Muslim communities not only contributed to, but led the way in, many fields, would form a vital part of our education. But it seems not. And, as a result, some people are still questioning whether or not Muslims can play a useful part in Europe, or the West generally. Perhaps those young Muslims who are often described as marginalised and, therefore, vulnerable to radicalisation, would feel less alienated if they were taught of the great contributions their ancestors made to the world. At the same time, those non-Muslims brought up on a diet of anti-Islamic news might feel differently about their Muslim neighbours if they could see this side of their culture, which has been kept well hidden for so long. Yet we prefer to continue peddling stories which reinforce ideas of Western superiority, and thereby continue to bolster assumptions about the inferiority of Muslims, while making young Muslims believe that they really are alien to, and therefore have little stake in, this advanced society.

One popular myth that continues to hold the imagination of millions is that of the Renaissance, and the preceding Dark Ages. The received history is that the Renaissance originated in Italy in about the 14th century, and that it came out of ideas from Florence in the late 13th century. It is still a widely held belief that it was essentially a European Christian phenomenon. And, of course, Renaissance literally means "rebirth", which further reinforces the impression that it arose almost out of nothing, that Christian European minds simply awoke from their slumber. Although those responsible were Christians, the origins of the Renaissance could really be attributed to more secular-minded Humanists, such as Dante. And it was the influx of eastern scholars after the fall of Constantinople in the 15th century that was an impetus for the Humanist Movement; those Eastern scholars brought with them important books and manuscripts, and introduced them to Greek scholarship. It was Europe's good fortune that the curtain could finally come down on an era characterised by religion and superstition. Although this view of the Dark Ages has now been revised in some circles, the fact is that, not so long ago, it was regularly taught.

In this chapter, we shall consider what was going on in the Muslim world while Europe was in the Dark Ages, and what impact, if any, it may have had on the Renaissance. Was the Renaissance a "rebirth" out of nothing? Or was it influenced by a tradition of rational thought and learning which had already existed for hundreds of years? As we shall see, the Muslim world from the 8th to the 15th centuries had some outstanding success stories, and, not for nothing, were the 12th and 13th centuries regarded as Islam's Golden Age. After the death of the Prophet in the 7th century, the spread of Islam brought Muslims into contact with other civilisations and cultures. Rather than ignoring the achievements of those cultures, the Muslims voraciously devoured the learning they were encountering, spurred on by their Holy Book, which described the search for knowledge as a religious duty. For example, encounters with India brought Muslims into contact with, amongst other things, Indian numerals. They took this knowledge on board and developed it, thus creating the system of Arabic numerals that we now use in the West.

Muslims from the Arabian peninsula were not only coming into contact with contemporary knowledge from other civilisations, but also discovering the ancient knowledge of the Greeks. Again, their Islamic faith did not prevent Muslims from absorbing what these "pagan" texts had to offer by way of knowledge, and using them as a basis for further study and development (a far cry, perhaps, from modern day attitude towards knowledge in some parts of the Muslim world). It is no secret that Greek learning came to the West as a result of the translations of the Arabs. (Often, in fact, Jewish scholars were involved in the process, as they were able to translate Arabic translations of Greek texts into Hebrew, thereby enabling later Latin scholars to translate into Latin from the Hebrew.) Similarly, papermaking came to Europe from China, again as a result of the Islamic expansion eastwards. The underlying theme in these interactions is not just a willingness on the part of the Muslims to receive other bodies of knowledge, but also a desire to develop the knowledge further. There are those who have erroneously reduced the role of the Arabs to simply that of translation. But even a cursory glance at some of their achievements reveals this to be false.

The Muslims used classical texts as a starting point

and, under the patronage of many generous Caliphs, were able to improve upon them. Muslim countries at the time boasted wealth as well as military power, which enabled them to attract and fund the scholars carrying out such work. Significantly, such funding was not provided on an informal, ad hoc basis, but constituted part of wider educational initiatives that included the establishing of universities, libraries and observatories; it was partly the abundance of such facilities that attracted scholars from around the Muslim world. The first university, in fact, was established in Cairo, while Baghdad was similarly pioneering with hospitals. (It is interesting to note that scientific experimentation was even used to decide the location of the main Baghdad hospital: pieces of meat were hung at various points around the city, and their rate of putrefaction monitored in order to work out the best place to build a hospital.)

The Bayt al Hikmah (House of Wisdom) in Baghdad, and the libraries of Cordoba and Damascus, contained thousands of manuscripts which were available to the public at a time when the cities of Europe could only muster a few hundred in the best of their private collections. One of the most impressive European libraries was that of the monastery of St Gall, yet its few volumes pale into insignificance when one considers that even the 13th-century observatory at Maragheh in Iran had up to 40,000 volumes.

There was a thirst for knowledge in the Muslim world of the Middle Ages, and a culture of scientific and technological achievement. There is much to lament in the Muslim world today, but it is not just for nostalgic reasons that we should recall the achievements of the Golden Age. They were real successes which not only led to Muslims being pre-eminent for centuries in the field of science, but also laid the foundations of the later successes of Europe and Western civilisation.

There are far too many noteworthy Muslim scientists, scholars and thinkers of the period for me to name here.

Perhaps a more useful approach would be to take a few areas and look at what Muslims achieved in each during the period, and then consider what the legacy of those achievements may have been. Of course, Muslim thinkers were by no means restricted to particular disciplines, but for present purposes the subjects we shall take a closer look at are mathematics, astronomy, chemistry and medicine.

Mathematics formed the basis of many of the achievements of the period we are considering – a fact which was once again precipitated by the Quran which, for example, laid out intricate rules relating to inheritance, whose implementation required complex mathematics. One of the earliest civilisations with which Islam came into contact was the Persian Empire, and it was largely from the Persians that the Muslims absorbed their knowledge of mathematics, which, in turn, the Persians had obtained from the Indians. The Arabs, as we have seen, referred to their numeric system as "Indian numerals"; the phrase "Arabic numerals" merely reflects the fact that Europe learned from Islamic scholarship. For the Arabs, however, it was not simply a system to learn, imitate and benefit from. It was something to apply their minds to, and to develop with their own original thinking.

We find, therefore, that although the numbers one through to nine evolved from Hindu-Buddhist works, it took an Arab scholar in the 9th century, Sind ibn Ali, to develop the system further and introduce decimal fractions. (In fact, although the concept of the zero pre-dates the Muslims, the word itself is derived from the Arabic *sifr*, which became *zefiro* in Italian, later shortened to zero.) The 9th century saw an amazing array of Muslim mathematical talent. As well as Sind ibn Ali, there was his colleague al-Khwarizmi, and also al-Kindi. Al-Kindi is difficult to label simply a mathematician, given his ability in the fields of philosophy, optics, medicine, chemistry and musical theory, but his book, *On the Use of the Indian Numerals*, played a significant part in the introduction of Arabic-Indian numerals to Europe.

The greatest of all Muslim mathematicians was undoubtedly Muhammad ibn Musa al-Khwarizmi – al-Khwarizmi for short – who lived from circa 780 to circa 850 CE. He was Persian by birth, and took up a place in Baghdad's House of Wisdom. Like so many Muslim scholars of that era, his expertise spanned several disciplines; and yet, despite his works in the fields of astronomy and geography, posterity rightly records him first and foremost as a mathematician. Today, few might appreciate that the word algorithm is derived from his name, but his contribution to the language of mathematics did not end there. One of his major works was entitled *al-Kitab al-mukhtasar fi hisab al-jabr wa'l muqabala* (*The Compendious Book on Calculation by Completion and Balancing*), and it is from this that we get the word "algebra". This was the first systematic solution of linear and quadratic equations in Arabic, and was based on intuitive geometric arguments, using just words, rather than the more abstract symbolic notation with which we are now familiar.

Al-Khwarizmi's work on algebra was revolutionary,

but he was also responsible for other significant developments. His book, *Kitāb al-Jam'wa-l-tafrīq bi-ḥisāb al-Hind* (*The Book of Addition and Subtraction According to the Hindu Calculation*), which was translated into Latin, was also instrumental in introducing to Europe the system of Arabic numerals based on the earlier work by the Indians. One criticism of the legacy of the Indians was that there was little by way of commentary included in their works. The Arabs, on the other hand, had no qualms about commenting on and explaining fully what they were setting out, and Al-Khwarizmi went to great lengths in his exposition of the Indian techniques, as well as his explanations of the zero. He is further said to have calculated the value of pi to 14 decimal places, as well as calculating the circumference of the Earth.

Like so many of the Muslim scholars of the Middle Ages, al-Khwarizmi's success was not limited to one field. In geography, he was able to correct the length of the Mediterranean in the ancient texts of Ptolemy. In astronomy, his "zij", or astronomical tables, devised new ways to track the movements of the sun, moon and five known planets. They were translated into Latin by Adelard of Bath, and formed the basis of all future planetary tables. Al Khwarizmi also developed a sundial which could be used at any latitude to tell the correct time, and which many mosques eventually installed to help with calculating correct times of prayer. He also seems to have developed several versions of the quadrant, a competitor of the astrolabe. Both were analogue computers that used sky positions to tell time and location. And, most remarkably, he achieved all this in the 9th century.

The same century also produced another Muslim

astronomer and mathematician, Muhammad ibn Jabir al-Harrani al-Battani (858–929 CE), or Albategnius in Latin, who carried on where al-Khwarizmi left off. Perhaps the greatest difficulty with al-Battani is deciding whether to put him with the mathematicians or the astronomers, such was the significance of his work in both fields. Although he was an astronomer, who in the 9th century calculated the length of the year as 365 days, 5 hours, 48 minutes and 24 seconds (in the year 2000 it was calculated to be 365 days, 5 hours, 48 minutes and 45 seconds), and produced work in that field of such import that he was later quoted by Copernicus, Kepler and Galileo, al-Battani is included here for his pioneering work on trigonometry.

By the 10th century, Islamic mathematicians were using all six trigonometric functions, had created tables of their values, and were applying them to problems in spherical geometry. Al-Battani was the first person to use the expression "sine" and "cosine" (*watar ma yabqa li-taman*). He discovered trigonometrical ratios, and improved Ptolemy's astronomical calculations by replacing geometrical methods with trigonometry. He provided ingenious solutions to problems of spherical trigonometry by using orthographic projection. He used trigonometric ratios as we use them today, and was the scientist who first replaced the use of Greek chords by sines, as well as developing the concept of the cotangent.

The problem of classifying Muslim scientists is particularly apparent when we move to the 11th century and consider Omar Khayyam (1048–1131 CE). In the West, he is best remembered as the author of the *Rubaiyat*, a collection of poems, or quatrains, which were famously translated into English by Edward Fitzgerald. The breadth of his achievements, however, can be gauged by the fact that in 1079 he calculated the length of the solar year to be 365.24219858156 days, shy by fractions of a second of the 365.242190 calculated in the 21st century with the aid of the Hubble space telescope. In fact, his "year" was more accurate than that of the Gregorian calendar, which followed 500 years later and which we still use today. Khayyam was a mathematician, astronomer and physicist who, amongst other works, authored the *Treatise on the Demonstration of Problems of Algebra* in which we find the first complete treatment of the solution of cubic equations. In addition to his mathematical achievements, he found the time to write the *Sharh-i Mushkil min Kitab al-Musiqi*, in which he deals with the mathematical structures of music.

So often, the greatest mathematicians of the Muslim world were also its greatest astronomers. Even this, however, is an unduly restrictive description; it was extremely rare that such scholars would limit themselves to just one or two subjects. Astronomy was a regular specialism, perhaps in no small part due to the Quran, which exhorted its readers to observe the stars in the sky. And observe they did. One of the greatest Muslim astronomers was the polymath Abu Rayhan al-Biruni (973–1048 CE), and although almost half of his 146 works were about mathematics and astronomy, his other works highlight his expertise as an anthropologist, geographer, ethnographer, physicist and pharmacologist. As a geographer, for example, he detailed the processes of determining longitude and latitude in his *Taḥdidnihāyāt al-amākin li-taṣḥīḥmasāfātal al-masākin* (*Determination of the Coordinates of Places for the Correction of Distances Between*

Cities), as well as discussing the formation of mountains and fossils.

One of al-Biruni's greatest contributions to the field of astronomy was to draw a distinction between astronomy and astrology. The latter was immensely popular at the time, but al-Biruni, in his *Al-Tafhīm li-awāʾilṣināʿat al-tanjīm* (*Elements of Astrology*), voiced his reservations about the subject, and his preference for the more rational arguments of astronomy. He devoted most of his work to mathematics, astronomy and geography, as well as the manufacture of the astrolabe. As long ago as the 11th century, he was arguing that it might be possible for the Earth to rotate on its own axis. In 1030, he wrote his masterpiece on astronomy, *Qanun al Masudi Fil Haiwal-Najum*, a truly encyclopaedic work of science, which contains collections of 23 observations of equinoxes, beginning with observations made by Ptolemy, and ending with original observations of his own. In this book he also discussed several theorems of astronomy, trigonometry, and solar, lunar and planetary motions.

Another important astronomer and all round scholar in the Islamic world was Muhammad ibn Nasir al-Din al-Tusi (1201–1274). At this stage in our journey through these scholars, it is somewhat unsurprising that we find that al-Tusi numbered among his areas of expertise philosophy, mathematics, medicine and biology. But he is best remembered for his contributions to astronomy. He was born in Persia just as it was about to fall victim to the invading Mongols. Al-Tusi, however, subsequently accepted a position to be the Mongol Hulagu Khan's scientific advisor, and it was in this influential role that he was able to lobby successfully for the funding to build an observatory at Maragheh, the

Ilkhanate capital, in modern day Azerbaijan. This was not only an observatory, but also one of the foremost libraries in the 13th century, and became a crucial centre from which knowledge was traded with the Chinese. (It was from this observatory that al-Shirazi later gave the first accurate explanation of the rainbow, an explanation that was further expanded upon by his student al-Farisi.)

From Maragheh, al-Tusi was able to produce the zij Ilkhani (Ilkhan astronomical tables), which were relied upon for centuries due to their accuracy. Al-Tusi was a prolific writer, and it was his *Al-Tadhkira-fi 'ilm al Hayah* (*Treatise on Astronomy*) which contained an astronomical-mathematical breakthrough that came to be known as the Tusi Couple. This re-evaluated and improved upon the ancient planetary models of Ptolemy by creating a system in which all planetary orbits were described by uniform circular motion. Its significance can be seen in the fact that it paved the way for the later work of Copernicus; references to it can be found in his writings. Also in al-Tusi's treatise we find a description of the Milky Way as containing a "very large number of small, tightly-clustered stars, which, on account of their concentration and smallness, seem to be cloudy patches, because of this, it was likened to milk in colour". This model of the Milky Way was later proved by Galileo.

Al-Tusi derived his appellation from the fact that he was born in Tus in Persia, but he was not the only notable Muslim scholar from that ancient city. Some 500 years earlier, Jabir ibn Hayyan (721–815 CE), whose name was later Latinised to Geber, was born there, and achieved such renown that many regard him as the father of modern chemistry. Although there are disputes about the authorship of many of the works attributed to him, there is little doubt that he made a significant contribution to the development of chemistry in the Western world. He placed great emphasis on the empirical method, stating that, "the first essential in chemistry is that you should perform practical work and conduct experiments"; it was this approach that paved the way for the eventual departure of chemistry from the less scientific and more esoteric alchemy. (This theme was picked up by his successor, the renowned philosopher Yaqub ibn Ishaq al-Kindi (circa 800–873 CE), who opposed the belief prevalent in alchemy that base metals could be turned into precious ones.) Various distillation processes are attributed to Jabir ibn Hayyan, as well as the discovery of nitric acid and hydrochloric acid, and also a substantial furthering of the knowledge and use of the alkali (al-qaly) and alembic (al-inbiq). As with many Muslim scientists, his works were not just theoretical discussions but, in fact, had very practical applications. He was an expert in applied science and an innovator in areas as diverse as dyeing hair and rustproofing metal.

Perhaps, however, the greatest legacy of Muslim scientists is in the field of medicine. For centuries, the work of Muslim physicians was regarded as the supreme authority when it came to the treatment of physical ailments. The few such physicians we shall consider lived between the 9th and the 13th centuries, but their influence extends much further. Our first physician – and the greatest, according to some critics – was the Persian Muhammad ibn Zakariya al-Razi (864–930 CE). He is reputed to have authored some 200 works on all aspects of medicine, and is famous for, amongst other things, being responsible for a number of significant medical "firsts". For example, he is regarded as the first to scientifically describe, and distinguish between, smallpox and measles in his *Kitab al-Judari w'al Hasabah* (*The Book of Smallpox and Measles*). He was the first to write about allergies and immunology, and discovered allergic asthma. He provided the first medical manual for the general public, and was the first to use opium for anaesthetic purposes. These were all incredible achievements for his time but just as important, if not more so, was his actual approach to his profession. He was unrelenting in his attacks on those he regarded as medical charlatans (which, to be fair, was probably most of those professing to know about medicine in the 9th century), and he was insistent that there be a scientific basis for any proposed cure. This attitude went hand in hand with his enthusiasm for continuing professional development and his insistence on medical ethics.

Various centres of scientific excellence developed in the Muslim world. Major cities such as Damascus, Cairo and Baghdad became places of great learning and practice. Further west in Spain, in the 10th century, Cordoba – "the ornament of the world" – was the birthplace of many a scholar, and not just the Muslims we are presently concerned with, but also such luminaries as the Jewish scholar Moses Maimonides. It could also boast as one of its sons Abu al -Qasim al-Zahrawi (936–1013 CE), known as Albucasis in the West, and regarded by many as the "father of modern surgery". He was an expert in dentistry, pharmacy and general surgery, but some of his most famous achievements were in the area of obstetrics. He was the first physician to describe an ectopic pregnancy, and he invented a pair of obstetric forceps which were used to remove foetuses that had perished in the womb. According to surgeons at the present day Cordoba Hospital, they are still in use.

Al-Zahrawi was also the author of the leading textbook on surgery in Europe for some five centuries, the *Method of Medicine*, or the *Kitab al-Tasrif*, which was translated by Gerard of Cremona in the 12th century. This work was made up of 30 volumes, and included the first accurate description of haemophilia. He was also responsible for the first documentation of the pathology of hydrocephalus. Al-Zahrawi deserves the credit for a number procedures that took on the names of those who came many centuries after him. For example, he was the first to describe an obstetric delivery position which later came to be known as the "Walcher position", named after the 19th-century German obstetrician. Similarly, the 19th-century Swiss physician Emil Kocher, lends his name to a procedure to reduce the anterior dislocation of the shoulder, but, in actual fact, the "Kocher manoeuvre" was described in al-Zahrawi's *al-Tasrif* over a thousand years earlier. He was also the first to use catgut sutures, the first to undertake exploratory surgery, and an early proponent of mastectomies.

A slightly unconventional method of recording the fame of medieval scholars is to name a crater on the Moon after them. Abu Ali al-Hasan ibn al-Haytham (965–1040 CE), known as Alhazen in the West, was one such contributor to the naming of lunar craters. Although he is generally described as a polymath, and achieved much in several scientific fields, for present purposes it is his contribution to the field of optics that commands our attention. He authored over 200 works, but his seven volumes on optics laid the foundations for the mathematical and optical theories later used by Galileo and Copernicus. Ibn al-Haytham was the first scientist to argue that vision is a phenomenon which takes place in the brain rather than the eyes. Contrary to accepted thought at the time, he proved that light rays do not emanate from the eyeball of the viewer and, indeed, went on to provide one of the earliest accurate descriptions of how the eyeball actually works. He also proved that light travels in straight lines, and so great was his understanding of this field that he began to build a camera obscura some five centuries before Leonardo da Vinci. (Incidentally, the law of refraction, also known as Snell's Law, or Descartes' Law, after the Dutch astronomer Willebrord Snellius, and the French scientist Descartes, both of whom lived in the 17th century, was, in fact, first accurately described by Ibn Sahl in 10th-century Baghdad.)

A few years after the birth of al-Haytham in what is now Iraq, another child was born, not too far away, in Iran. He would go on to be described as "the most famous scientist of Islam"; his full name was Abu ᶜAli al-Ḥusayn ibnᶜAbd Allah ibn Sina (980–1037 CE), or Avicenna in the West. He was another polymath who subsequently had the almost mandatory lunar crater named after him, and, having memorised the Quran by the age of 10, he went on to distinguish himself primarily in the fields of medicine, mathematics and philosophy. His major medical works include the *Book of Healing* (*Kitab al-Shifa*) and the *Canon of Medicine* (*Al-Qanun fi al-Tibb* or the *Laws of Medicine*). The latter was a 14-volume work which became the standard medical textbook in Europe for some five centuries, and was used in

French universities as late as the 17th century. It provided scientific explanations and classifications of diseases which practitioners in Europe at the time insisted were simply Divine punishment. It was translated into Latin by Gerard of Cremona in the 12th century, and was published in Venice in 1493, Rome in 1593, and was used at the famous medical school of Salerno.

Ibn Sina was another Muslim scientist who insisted on clinical trials and experimentation, and provided the study and practice of medicine with a formal scientific structure. He, too, refuted alchemy and astrology, preferring the more logical and empirical approaches of chemistry and astronomy. He established scientific rules for the testing of drugs which were so thorough that they still form the basis of clinical pharmacology a thousand years later. He is regarded by many as the first to explain formally the spread of contagious diseases and to outline the benefits of quarantine. He emphasised clinical trials and, at a time when most of Europe rejected the view, he insisted that tuberculosis was infectious. He also began the first documented exploration of what later became known as psychotherapy in his discussions of the mind-body connection, and the role of mental issues in physical ailments. He described meningitis, discussed anaesthetics and elaborated upon bone fractures and how best to heal them. Once again we find that his work was not purely theoretical, but extended to the invention of medical instruments, such as the one he used to probe the tear duct.

Ibn Sina undoubtedly left behind an enduring legacy, but one scholar who had the stature to criticise his more speculative assertions was Abu Marwan Abd al-Malik ibn

Zuhr (1091–1161 CE), known as Avenzoar in the West. He was born in Seville and graduated from the medical university at Cordoba. Unlike most of the Muslim scholars whom we have considered, Ibn Zuhr confined himself to just one discipline – medicine – but this enabled him to excel as a clinician, physician and parasitologist. He was the first to comprehensively describe parasites and the diseases they cause, such as scabies. He knew the human anatomy in detail, having become an expert at dissecting cadavers. He was also the first to test different medicines on animals before administering them to humans. His experimentation on animals, in particular goats, also led to his formalising and perfecting the practice of tracheotomies and direct feeding through the gullet where normal feeding was not possible. Although he was the author of many works, only three of his major books remain: the *Book of Simplification Concerning Therapeutics and Diet*, the catchily titled *Book of the Middle Course Concerning the Reformation of Souls and Bodies*, and the more manageable *Book of Foodstuffs*. Aside from his medical achievements, he should be remembered for persuading his daughter and granddaughter to go into medicine – perhaps a surprising initiative given that he lived in the 12th century, and one which some Muslims would do well to adopt in the 21st.

Ibn Zuhr was also notable for being a teacher of the great Averroes, or Abu'l Walid ibn Rushd (1126–1198 CE). His name is certainly known in the West and, along with Ibn Sina, he even "merited" a place in Limbo in Dante's *Divine Comedy*. He is mainly remembered for his philosophical work – in particular, his rationalist approach, which dramatically altered the landscape of Western thought five centuries before the thinking of René Descartes. He did, however, originally study medicine and law, and his major work on medicine was *Al-Kulliyyat* or *Generalities*. It was translated into Latin as the *Colliget* in Padua in 1255 CE, and the first edition was printed in Venice in 1492 CE. It is subdivided into seven further books – the *Anatomy of Organs, Health, Sickness, Symptoms, Drugs and Foods, Hygiene and Therapy* – and, together with Ibn Zuhr's work on therapeutics and diet, it was intended to form a comprehensive alternative medical text to Ibn Sina's *Canon*. Despite having authored a commentary on the *Canon*, Ibn Rushd will be remembered first and foremost as a philosopher. But this should in no way detract from his contribution to medicine, particularly in Muslim Spain.

The final character we shall mention while perusing Islamic scientific achievements is Ala al-Din ibn Nafis (1213–1288 CE), who was born in Damascus, and went on to become the head of Cairo hospital. He, too, wrote commentaries on the work of the great scholars of medicine such as Ibn Sina and Hunan ibn Ishaq, and produced his own treatises on ophthalmology, eye disease and diet. It is in his commentary on Ibn Sina's *Canon* that we find the first description of pulmonary circulation (the movement of blood from the heart to the lungs and back to the heart again), in which he corrected the hitherto accepted view, originating from the Greek physician Galen, that blood passes directly from the right side of the heart to the left. Ibn Nafis stated that the wall between the right and left ventricles of the heart is non-porous and that the blood must, therefore, pass by way of the lungs.

This view is believed to have been first promulgated in

Europe by Michael Servetus in 1553, Andreas Vesalius in 1555 and Realdo Colombo in 1559, who were all precursors of William Harvey, whose publication in 1628 is regarded as the definitive discovery of blood circulation. At its most charitable, this version of history holds that the European "discovery" was independent of Ibn Nafis' earlier work, of which it was completely ignorant. This may be true, but it requires a little more scrutiny, as it also has a bearing on our wider discussion of the significance of Muslim scientific achievement.

The relevant text by Ibn Nafis was found in the Prussian State Library in 1924, and the line has always been that the European scholars could not have known about it. History does record, however, that there was an Italian physician from Belluno near Padua by the name of Andrea Alpago, who lived in Syria for some time, where he encountered the work of Ibn Nafis – who, we recall, was born in Damascus. He translated Ibn Nafis' work into Latin, and it was published in Venice in 1547, some 26 years after his death. Michael Servetus had spent time in Italy, and, in 1553, published *Christianismi Restitutio*, the *Restitution of Christianity*, in which he put forward the theory of pulmonary circulation. As its name suggests, this was a theological work, and a highly controversial one, as it was regarded as anti-Trinitarian and heretical. It was, therefore, destroyed. Few copies remained, so, unsurprisingly, the pulmonary circulation part did not gain too much publicity.

In 1555, Andreas Vesalius, a Flemish anatomist, published a revised edition of his work *De Humani Corporis Fabrica* (*On the Fabric of the Human Body*), in which he disputed Galen's view that the wall between the ventricles of the heart is porous. Vesalius had also lived briefly in Venice, before moving to Padua to study for his doctorate, which he received in 1537, and, after which, he became the Chair of Surgery and Anatomy at the university. A colleague, or perhaps more likely, a rival, of Vesalius at Padua was Realdo Colombo – a surgeon and professor of anatomy at Padua from 1544 to 1559. He also shares the title of the "discoverer" of pulmonary circulation, as does a student of his called Juan Valverde de Amusco. Accusations of plagiarism abounded between these three scholars. Now, it may seem at first blush that the work of the Englishman William Harvey, published in 1628, was entirely unconnected to, and independent of, these Italian shenanigans. But a bit more research reveals that Harvey himself studied at the University of Padua between 1599 and 1602. It may well be the case that the work of Ibn Nafis did, in fact, remain unknown to Europe until 1924. But it is worth entertaining the idea that his work had filtered through to the universities of Italy, and from there been disseminated elsewhere.

※ ※ ※

This brings us neatly to the significance of the above-mentioned Muslim scientific achievements. The purpose of this chapter was never to bask in the glare of past glories, but, first and foremost, to educate and inform. And not just to educate and inform non-Muslims, but also Muslims themselves who are, all too often, sadly unaware of their own history, and the achievements which can properly be attributed to their ancestors. It is painful to bring to mind just how little of the above history is taught in Western schools, and it requires no great intellectual leap to anticipate what the results of this lack of information are likely to be. Science is portrayed as the preserve of the civilised West; the rest of the world, particularly the Muslim world, lags behind. It was, it is implied, always thus. Muslim children grow up unaware that their ancestors made huge contributions to scientific knowledge, and non-Muslim children see no alternative to the negative stereotypes regularly depicted by the media. For this reason alone, it is vital that Islamic scientific achievements are recalled and highlighted.

When they are, some underlying themes quickly become apparent. Perhaps the most important is that Muslim scientific success occurred in regions of political stability and material wealth. There was an undoubted thirst for knowledge, but quenching it was made easier by the willingness of wealthy and powerful rulers to sponsor those engaged in academic endeavour. Once centres of learning were established in cities from Cordoba in the West to Samarkand in the East, taking in Cairo, Damascus and Baghdad along the way, they were bound to attract the greatest minds, secure in the knowledge that their efforts would be supported. Similarly, today, the cause of scientific progress is furthered most in those countries that not only have the means to fund it, but are also able to provide physical security and political stability to those who want to pursue it. It is no accident that in contemporary Muslim societies most scientific progress is taking place in countries such as Turkey and Malaysia, where there is relative prosperity and political stability.

Another theme that becomes apparent is the extent to which ideas cross-pollinated. In the days before copyright and patenting issues, it was accepted, certainly among

Muslims, that there should be no monopoly over knowledge: the Creator made it freely available to all who sought it. Muslim scholars readily absorbed the works of the Greeks and Indians, and the technology of the Persians and Chinese, and regarded it as their duty to develop this knowledge and pass it on to others. Although the term "Arabic numerals", for example, has come to be accepted now, a thousand years ago the Arabs themselves referred to the numbers as Indian, or Hindi, thereby acknowledging where they had inherited this system from.

Yet it was not just when accepting received wisdom that knowledge was shared. Perhaps the best example of this is the success story of Al-Andalus, or Muslim Spain, a thousand or so years ago. Cordoba was, at one time, probably the biggest, cleanest, most learned and technically advanced city in the world. A major cause of its success was that it provided an environment in which cooperation between Muslims, Christians and Jews was valued and encouraged. This is how it was able to produce no less a Jewish scholar than Moses Maimonides, and in Ibn Rushd or Averroes, a Muslim philosopher whose commentaries on Aristotle significantly influenced the thinking of Thomas Aquinas. (Perhaps it is also worth noting, albeit regrettably, that their respective communities have criticised each of these scholars for their inclusive outlook.)

But the most important, and controversial, idea arising from this journey through the scientific successes of medieval Muslims relates to the role that such successes played in creating the modern West. We are all familiar with the phrase, "Arabic numerals", and we know why our numbers are described as Arabic. We are perhaps less aware, however, of the origins of words such as algebra, zero, cipher, almanac, zenith, azimuth, alchemy, alcohol, alkali, elixir, syrup, bazaar, tariff and arsenal: all of them come from Islamic words. It is important to note here the significance of language in the development of civilisations and cultures. Only a moment's thought about the cultural supremacy of the West today, and the role that the English language plays in this, is sufficient to make our point. There is a reason that these Arabic words found their way into Western languages, and it is simply this: they were part of the vocabulary of the academics and experts who were discussing the major ideas of the day.

And it was not just words which the Muslims provided for the West. We have already noted how certain ideas that were later adopted by Europeans did, in fact, originate in earlier Islamic thought. The names of William Harvey, Snell, Walcher and Kocher, may be the ones we recall, but that should not blind us to the fact that much original scientific thinking had been going on for centuries before the likes of them emerged on the scene. To be fair, the Western scholars themselves were often happy to acknowledge the efforts of their predecessors; it was their followers who gave the impression that Western achievements were born out of an intellectual vacuum. Our discussions of astronomy may begin and end with Copernicus, but the man himself was happy to quote Al-Battani and Ibn al-Haytham.

We may believe that one of the great achievements of Western civilisation was to rid the scientific world of its irrational religious superstitions, which hampered its progress, but again the reality is different. One after another, Muslim scientists emphasised the importance of experimentation and the empirical method. The backlash of the Church against science was not a phenomenon familiar to the Muslim scholars who were actively encouraged by their faith in their scientific pursuits.

5

Or in need of anger management?

Muslims seem to be an angry bunch, don't they? There is a perception, which is understandable to some extent, that all Muslims ever do is gripe, moan, demonstrate, protest and ultimately lash out violently. Unreasonable and uncivilised, they contrive to cover up their own shortcomings by constantly blaming "the West" for their problems, without ever mentioning the corruption, lack of political freedoms and wanton violence which, amongst other flaws, characterise their own societies. Muslims, as individuals, have a persecution complex which leads them to believe they are always the victims of discrimination because of their religion. They wilfully cut themselves off from the rest of society, and thus lose out on opportunities which may otherwise present themselves.

The undercurrent of such negative perceptions of Muslims is, of course, that the actions of Muslims have no legitimate basis whatsoever. Is this, however, entirely true? Are Muslims completely unreasonable, or are some of their grievances real, and their complaints justified? These are some of the questions we need to ask in order to ascertain whether or not Muslims need to be collectively booked on to an anger-management course.

It is very rare that I bemoan the state of the Islamic world in the 21st century and blame it on the Crusades. But there is a feeling expressed by some that Muslims have very long memories, and have neither forgotten, nor forgiven, the Christian Crusaders who invaded the Middle East; the events may well have taken place almost a thousand years ago, but they are supposedly etched very clearly in the minds of all Muslims, and explain the resentment of the West in the Muslim world. Well, in case anybody is wondering, I am not holding the Crusades against my Christian friends, nor am I waiting for any form of redress. The Crusades were undoubtedly a tragic chapter in the history of Christian-Muslim relations, but they are not a regular topic of conversation in Muslim households. At least, they were not until George W. Bush famously used the word prior to invading Iraq, thereby reminding Muslims that even if *they* had forgotten the Crusades, the descendants of those who were responsible for them had not.

When Pope Urban II called for the Crusades in 1095, he set off a train of events that was to leave an indelible mark on the Middle East. At the time, Christianity was split between the eastern Byzantine Church and the western Latin Church, and, it is fair to say, there was not necessarily a great deal of trust between the two. The Crusades were one way for the Pope to gain supremacy over the whole of the Church by ending the savage persecution of Christians by the infidel Muslims, and regaining Jerusalem in the process. The problem with this, however, was that there was no savage persecution of Christians by Muslims.

Jerusalem had been in Muslim hands for almost 500 years, and in that time the majority of the population had remained Christian. It may be somewhat surprising that, at a stage in history during which general slaughter was not uncommon, Muslims did not compel the Christians of Jerusalem to convert to Islam, or face the sword. But this only reflects the religious tolerance enjoined upon them in the Quran, which reminds them that there is "no compulsion in faith". The ruling Muslims, the Fatimids of Egypt, were fairly tolerant for their time. This was happily overlooked by the Pope, and those who followed his command were barely concerned with the niceties of religious faith, as was amply manifested in their conduct en route to the Holy Land when they attacked fellow Christians as well as, sadly rather more predictably, any Jewish communities they encountered. Once they eventually arrived in Jerusalem, the manner in which they took the city was so unnecessarily brutal that the accounts of their horses being knee deep in the bodies of "infidel" men, women and children (and animals) bear testimony to this day.

Following this, there was a Crusader presence in the Holy Land for hundreds of years. During which time, a number of Muslims regrouped, and eventually reconquered parts of the region – most famously, Saladin captured Jerusalem in 1187. It is fair to say that these reconquests were not exactly met with displeasure by the local Eastern Christians. They may well have believed in the same Christ as their Latin brethren, but they looked and behaved similarly to their Muslim counterparts – a fact which had not pleased the newly arrived Crusaders, and certainly did not increase the trust between the two branches of the faith. (Even today the Coptic Christians of Egypt refer to God as Allah; one wonders how they would be received by the evangelical right wing of Christianity in the West.)

Saladin is, of course, a hero to Muslims for his recapture of Jerusalem, but he is also legendary in the West as a chivalrous warrior. He was famed for his generosity and humanity, releasing prisoners of war at a time when it was customary to execute them. Richard the Lionheart himself, for example, ordered the massacre of 2,700 survivors of the Muslim garrison of Acre. The difference between the conduct of Muslims and Christians during the Crusades is one of the legacies of this chapter of history, certainly as far as Muslims are concerned. They contrast the way in which Saladin captured Jerusalem, leaving unharmed all women and children, with the manner in which it fell in 1099, and the wanton bloodshed that followed at the hands of the invading Crusaders.

It serves the purposes of some, in both the Muslim and Christian camps, to depict the Crusades as a war between Islam and Christianity itself. They insist that the two faiths could not happily co-exist, and that violence was the only way to determine which should dominate. This point of view has always been resisted by other followers of the faith, who regard God as the ultimate arbiter of religious disputes, rather than those who carry the bigger sticks. Invariably, what such people also recognise is that, more often than not, so-called "religious" disputes are a convenient way of disguising wars with other agendas. Pope Urban II's motives were not as simple as protecting the faith, any more than were the motives of the Crusaders themselves. We find this pattern recurring constantly in history: some sort of religious pretext is used as a cover for a war that is really motivated by greed and the desire for political power. The Crusades themselves were really motivated by political and financial considerations; they were wars of colonisation, in which the colonisers sought to impose their civilisation on the subjected populations. They were not the first such wars, nor would they be the last, especially as far as Muslims were concerned, who would become all too familiar with subjugation by European Christians.

Almost every Muslim country has been colonised by Western powers at some stage – a situation which, for many such countries, did not change until the last fifty years or so. This has meant that the experiences of colonisation are much more relevant to most Muslims than those of the Crusades. Not only have they left a legacy in the colonised countries, but they continue to influence the relationship between Muslims and the West today. For example, the centuries-long involvement of the British in India ultimately led to the immigration to the United Kingdom of Pakistani workers, amongst others, in the post-war years (and without that immigration this book would not have been written). Similar patterns can be witnessed in other European countries. France had a colonial presence in Algeria from 1830 to 1962, as well as in Tunisia and Morocco, leading to its large North African immigrant population today. It subsequently colluded with the British in the partitioning of the Ottoman Empire, and French influence is still visible in Lebanon, where it carried out its "divide and rule" policy with some success. Britain's history of involvement in the region includes a period of direct military control of Iraq, as well as the later installation of kings it regarded as suitable for its purposes, which, of course, were not necessarily the purposes of the host nation. The British also had significant control of Egypt, including periods of indirect rule, when the apparent leader may have been the emir, sheikh or khedive, but the true power lay elsewhere.

There are some interesting parallels between the colonial period of history and contemporary global events, which highlight numerous lessons that ought to have been learned. Iraq is the obvious example. We continue to intervene, with scant regard for the wishes, or indeed the lives, of the indigenous population. The first Iraq war, in 1991, is now regarded as legally and morally justified (in part because the later one was so obviously not), yet few people remember the role that the American ambassador to Iraq, April Glaspie, played prior to the Iraqi invasion of Kuwait, which led to Western intervention. Before the invasion, Saddam Hussein held a meeting with Glaspie, in which he mentioned the "difficulty" he was having with Kuwait, and alleged that the Kuwaitis were illegally drilling for oil in Iraqi fields. Her response was to say that, as far as the United States was concerned, it was an internal matter for the Iraqis, upon which the United States had "no opinion".

One could well understand that Saddam Hussein – an ally of the United States who had attacked Iran at their instigation, and whom they had even armed – interpreted this response as a green light. Yet the military action that followed was unprecedented in its speed and scale. Numerous opportunities to forestall war were spurned by America, who seemed intent on taking this opportunity to destroy Iraq's military capability while testing out its own. Perhaps the most sickening episode was the "turkey shoot" towards the end of the conflict, when American soldiers gloated about wiping out thousands of *fleeing* Iraqi soldiers. One wonders how such events would have been reported had it been the other way round.

The approach to the invasion of 2003 clearly involved many more economies of truth than were required in 1991, but certain features remained the same. Naomi Klein, in *The Shock Doctrine* highlights how the same Western corporations profited from the war: $20 billion worth of contracts went to Halliburton alone. (Setting aside moral considerations for a moment, one can marvel at the genius of a system which generates huge profits by selling arms to make nations powerful, generates huge profits by using arms to destroy those nations, and generates huge profits from the contracts to rebuild the same nations after their destruction. "Win-win" does not even begin to describe this state of affairs.)

Another similarity between 2003 and 1991 was the callous indifference we displayed towards those whom we claimed to be seeking to save. Western championing of the Kurds was part of the build-up to the invasion of Iraq in 2003, yet, just as before, once our immediate objective had been achieved, that Kurdish homeland remained as elusive for the Kurds as it had always been. At this point, it is perhaps worth remembering the words of General F. S. Maude, Commander of British Forces, Baghdad, 19th March 1917: *"Our armies do not come into your cities and lands as conquerors or enemies, but as liberators... it is the hope and desire of the British people and the nations in alliance with them that the Arab race may rise once more to greatness and renown among the peoples of the earth."* This professed enthusiasm for "liberating" was presumably not intended to mean liberating their resources.

That was just a happy coincidence.

Events in Iraq showed how, so often, rulers in the Middle East are installed and removed at our behest, no matter what kind of democratic veneer is applied by our politicians in order to stave off domestic criticism. In the past, some of these Muslim countries looked to the West for support in achieving their own reforms and independence – from the Ottomans, for example – but then, as now, our support for democratic reforms did not take precedence over our colonial/national interests. From early 2011, a wave of pro-democracy demonstrations took place in Muslim countries from Tunisia to Syria, yet Western support was tempered to say the least, dependent on our interests rather than those of the demonstrators. NATO intervention in Libya, for example, was suspected of being based on our hatred of Gaddafi and/or love of his oil, rather than any democratic principle, and was always going to be contrasted with the policy of encouraging "stability" when similar anti-government demonstrations had taken place earlier in Egypt.

The number of civilian deaths that have occurred in Iraq from the time of the invasion in 2003 is estimated to be in the region of one million. We do not know the exact figure because no such record has ever been maintained (contrary to the norms of conduct in war). This sorry fact reflects the general lack of interest that the West has always shown the populations of such countries. It was Winston Churchill who made the infamous remark about not getting unduly squeamish over the use of chemical weapons on "savage tribes". He was a true British hero but, given that remark, it may come as no surprise that others around the world regard him with some antipathy. Churchill was referring to the use of such weapons on the people of Iraq, yet no irony was noted when the very same chemical weapons were used to justify the Iraq invasion. It is, of course, now old news that such weapons of mass destruction did not, in fact, exist in Iraq immediately prior to the invasion, but they certainly found their way there once the Western war effort was in full swing, as evidenced by their use by the "coalition" in Fallujah. This appalling episode received little attention in the West, and again many Muslims questioned how it would have been treated by the media if the victims had been non-Muslims in Europe or America. The suspicion in many quarters was that it would have received saturation coverage (although when Saddam Hussein himself used chemical weapons on the people of Halabja during the Iran-Iraq war, our condemnation was somewhat muted, perhaps understandably, given that he was then our ally and it was we who had armed him).

One would expect Muslims to feel aggrieved at being colonised or subjected to unwarranted military occupation or action. These were visible interventions which were more acceptable in an age when many Western powers were behaving similarly. Times change, however, and in the post-war years, imperialist ventures and colonialism came to be depicted as a thing of the past. Many countries of the developing world began to gain independence and, on the face of it, an era of autonomy and self-determination was being ushered in. It could be argued, however, that all that has changed is that direct intervention has became indirect, and physical colonisation has been replaced by cultural and economic colonisation. After all, why go to the expense and inconvenience of physically occupying and ruling a country if there are other ways of relieving it of its resources?

Resources – or, in other words, wealth – were ultimately what imperial Western powers were after. They competed with each other to gain mastery over the wealth of the world, whether in Africa and India in the past, or the Middle East and its oil resources in the present. Intervention – or in the eyes of some, interference – which fell short of direct military occupation became the preferred tactic. Tragically, and with a staggering degree of short-sightedness, little attention was paid to the potential consequences of such interventions. So, although the age of colonialism was ending, it did not mean for a moment that foreign lands would be in control of their own affairs.

Many Muslim countries, which had previously been colonised by European countries like Britain, France, Germany, Italy and others, looked forward to independence and took heart from that great success story across the Atlantic Ocean: America. That nation had fought for its own independence from the very same colonialism. It had not itself developed colonies around the world. And it had, in the 20th century, used its military might to safeguard the security of other nations under threat. Up until the middle of that century, the Muslim world had high regard for the United States, certainly as compared to the other powers they had encountered. Things were to change drastically for a variety of reasons. We shall look at Israel – perhaps the greatest grievance that Muslims hold against America – shortly, but its case is far from an isolated example of the US involving itself in the affairs of Muslims, and, indeed, their neighbours. The United States of America may insist it has no imperialist ambitions, may utter all the right words about democracy and freedom, but even a cursory look at its track record suggests that this picture is not entirely accurate.

One of the disadvantages of being part of a Western democracy is that our attention is diverted from any conflict by suited politicians who say all the right things while insidious secret services do all the wrong things. In fact, much of the time we, the populace, are oblivious to the fact that such secret services play a significant role at all, and are content to accept the headlines at face value. "National security" requirements mean that documents are classified for decades, so it is only much later that a clearer picture finally emerges. This, of course, assumes that those who are still around retain sufficient interest in the topic. The United States (and other so-called liberal democracies) are then revealed to have suppressed and opposed many a progressive movement around the globe.

Volumes have been written about the devastation wrought in Latin America with the encouragement and connivance of the US. But, for now, it is the Muslim world which is the focus of our attention, and it is a subject replete with examples of the Land of the Free subverting democracy and overthrowing regimes. In 1953, for example, democratically elected Iranian prime minister, Mossadeq, declared that the oil under Iranian soil belonged to Iran, but failed to realise that such talk was never going to endear him to Uncle Sam who, inevitably, decided it was best to get rid of him. Lest it be thought this was an isolated example, the USA did its best thereafter to ensure that no corner of the Muslim world (or, indeed, anywhere else) escaped the reach of its tentacles.

During the same decade, the United States attempted to

overthrow the Syrian government, and even to assassinate Nasser of Egypt. (The British and French, in collusion with Israel, also thought that the latter was a legitimate target. I still remember my shock at reading the *Observer*'s report in 1986 of Anthony Eden's role in the attempt against Nasser's life. Evidently, the 30-year rule could hide some pretty dastardly deeds.) There were Arab nationalist leaders at the time who attempted to remain neutral in the Cold War, but as far as the United States was concerned there was no such thing as neutral; you were either pro-American or you were Communist. Any nationalist sentiments were, by definition, not pro-American and, according to American logic, must have been Communist. This anti-Communist paranoia led to much death and destruction around the world, and Muslim countries were not exempt. General Kassem in Iraq had overthrown the monarchy and established a republic. He desired to remain neutral in the Cold War but, in helping to create OPEC (the Organisation of the Petroleum Exporting Countries, which undermined Western control over the marketing of the Middle East's oil), he had clearly indicated that he was serving the wrong national interest. This was sufficient reason for the British and Americans to back a coup against him.

Anti-Communist feeling motivated American policy in Indonesia, too, home to the world's largest Muslim population. Sukarno became the first Indonesian president in 1949, having previously been the leader of the movement to gain independence from the Netherlands. He nationalised many Dutch private holdings and, in doing so, proved that he put the interests of his own countrymen first. Despite their expressed intentions to counter Communism, it is evident from their actions that the Americans' primary goal was, as ever, to disrupt any socially progressive movement which might send out the wrong signals to others. All around the world, the USA intervened wherever it felt its business interests would suffer if the locals insisted on working to further their own interests and improve their quality of life, usually at the expense of Western corporations. Despite Sukarno jointly founding the Non-Aligned Movement (the clue is in the name), which attempted to remain neutral in the American-Soviet conflict, he was setting an example that the US could not tolerate. In 1966, he was overthrown by General Suharto, and the mass killing of "Communists" ensued, assisted in part by the US embassy helpfully providing lists of said Communists to the army.

In the 1970s, the United States participated in its occasional pastime of supporting the Kurds. The Kurdish people are predominantly Sunni Muslims, who inhabit the area where Turkey, Syria, Iran and Iraq meet. When the Ottoman Empire was carved up by the Treaty of Sèvres in 1920, the Kurds were promised independence, but when Ataturk came to power, he rejected the treaty and agreed with Iraq and Iran not to recognise an independent Kurdish state. Decades followed in which their struggle for independence lay dormant and their population suffered at the hands of the governments of the region. They found an unexpected ally in the United States, but soon realised their support was based upon political expedience rather than any principled desire to see an independent Kurdistan. It was that highly regarded combination of Richard Nixon and Henry Kissinger (hardly renowned for their ethical foreign policy, or ethical anything for that matter) which began to provide military aid to the Kurds of Iraq. This, however, was calculated to drain and distract Iraq and, thereby, serve the interests of their regional ally, the Shah of Iran. Once Iran and Iraq had come to terms in 1975, the Kurds were abandoned to their fate, and, sadly, not for the last time.

The Shah of Iran was a close friend of the West, the US in particular, and his deposition is a dramatic illustration of how America conducted itself on the world stage. The US had backed the Shah of Iran, as it had many other Middle Eastern dictators, but was so unconcerned with the rest of the Iranian population that it failed to notice that there was a popular movement gaining strength which would ultimately overthrow him in 1979, leaving his backers powerless. The exiled Ayatollah Khomeini returned a hero and, almost overnight, a whole country became anti-American, with repercussions that reverberate to this day. Following the Iranian Revolution, a CIA "village" was discovered in Tehran, yet one wonders what kind of "intelligence" they were gathering which caused them to miss an entire country turning against its ruler and his international sponsors.

Rather than learning from that episode, the US has continued to involve itself in the affairs of other countries by supporting dictators, coups and violence while being utterly uninterested in the wishes of the populations of those countries. The preaching of freedom and democracy continued to ring out, especially when targeted at rival/ enemy countries such as China, but when there have been genuine attempts to gain democratic rights in Egypt, for example, the foot-dragging on the part of the US has been painful to watch. Rather than rejoice in the spontaneous assertion of the Egyptians' desire for political freedoms

– something President Obama had openly called for in his address to the Muslims of the world in June 2009 – the Americans called for "stability", for which we can read "maintaining the pro-American stance of the dictator Hosni Mubarak".

Over thirty years after the Islamic Revolution in Iran, the CIA continues to act with impunity in neighbouring Pakistan, content that those in power in that country will be compliant, regardless of what the other 180 million people may think. The arrest of suspected CIA operative Raymond Davis in early 2011 for killing two Pakistanis further agitated a nation already frustrated at its impotence in the face of the American aggression perpetrated on its soil, and highlighted just how much licence to operate had been granted to the CIA by the Pakistani authorities. In fact, the Pakistani foreign minister resigned his position rather than give in to American/Pakistani government pressure to change the visa of Raymond Davis to a diplomatic one after he had been arrested. Here was a country which was an ally in the War on Terror, and had suffered greatly for being so, with some 35,000 people having been killed as of May 2011 (over ten times the death toll of 9/11). Yet, despite this, it was subjected to constant attacks by unmanned American drone aircraft, and vilified in the western media, regularly being described as a failed state and terrorist hotbed.

Such allegations resurfaced again in May 2011 when Osama Bin Laden was shot dead in Abbottabad in Pakistan. Initial reports claimed that he was living in a luxury compound, had been armed, had used his wife as a human shield, was shot while resisting "arrest", and that the whole episode was viewed by President Obama on a live video feed. Within days, this version was amended: the luxury compound was just a dwelling with no air-conditioning, Bin Laden was unarmed, he did not use his wife as a human shield, and it turned out the event was not watched by the US president, because the live feed went down for 25 minutes at the crucial time. Such details were lost in the fog of accusations being levelled at Pakistan about what it knew and when it knew it. They also did not serve to placate a sceptical Pakistani population, which again felt angered and humiliated at the flagrant breach of their national sovereignty while their own government did nothing. The actions of the Americans did little to convince other Muslims around the globe, who queried, amongst other things, why the most wanted man in the world was not arrested (especially if he was unarmed), why his wife was not detained by the Americans when surely she would have been able to provide much useful information, and why having dumped his body at sea, the Americans insisted this was to do with their concern for Muslim sensibilities. The latter point confirmed, for many Muslims, the contempt with which they were regarded by the US.

The media appeared keen to report on matters that reflected badly on Pakistan, but never to investigate any suggestions that there were deliberate attempts to destabilise it. One such suggestion was that, employing that classic imperialistic tactic of divide and rule, the USA was covertly supporting an independence movement in the province of Balochistan. Articles would appear in Western journals discussing such movements, thereby lending credence to them. Financial and military aid would then be sent in the full knowledge that this would at the very least lead to instability, and, if required, provide a pretext for direct military intervention. Of course, as this never made the Western press, it was deemed not to have occurred, and anybody bold enough to raise it was given no credence. After all, why on earth would the United States undermine its own allies? Those who posed this question seemed blissfully unaware of America's track record. Not for nothing has it been said that it is dangerous to be America's enemy, but not as dangerous as being its friend. The question also ignored the complex geopolitics of the area.

Balochistan is the largest province in Pakistan. It has vast, untapped reserves of minerals including copper, gold and platinum. It provides one-third of Pakistan's gas. It borders with Iran and the Helmand province in Afghanistan. It also contains the port of Gwadar, a Chinese-built facility which allows China's landlocked western provinces access to the sea, and thus the oil shipping lanes of the Straits of Hormuz. Travelling by road through Pakistan, China could transport goods to Gwadar in a day, saving itself the considerable time and expense of accessing the sea through its eastern borders. If ever a province was begging for American interference, it was Balochistan. Pakistani military officials, constantly maligned in the West as treacherous closet extremists, lament the fact that while they help the Americans fight the Taliban, at great cost to their own nation, they also have to deal with American and Indian support for a separatist movement in Balochistan.

As many Muslims see it, America deliberately destabilises countries in the Islamic world in order to keep them from developing. Doing so allows them to further their own imperialist agenda, and continue to proclaim their superiority due to their democratic credentials. Instability provides a ready-made excuse to intervene militarily as and when required, and, of course, helps keep defence budgets astronomically high, even though the threat from Communist Russia has long since subsided. An army of pro-Israel media "experts" uses such instability to present Israel in a glowing light, as an island of stability surrounded by undemocratic, violent, Muslim nations hell-bent on its destruction. Israel – which was hardly cheering for the Arab Spring in 2011 – never ceases to portray itself as the only democracy in the Middle East, conveniently ignoring both how the dictatorships arose in the first place, and the existence of countries such as Lebanon, or even Iran. It is perhaps as a result of those countries' democratic efforts that Israel has been so keen either to invade them or ensure that someone else, like the US, does. For years, the Israelis have highlighted the "threat" of Iran, despite the fact that in the 36 years since the Iranian Revolution, Iran has not invaded a single country. The same, of course, cannot be said for Israel – a fact that the Lebanese know only too well. Disappointingly for Israel, this has yet to result in an American invasion of Iran. But it is certainly not for want of trying.

The Israeli author Israel Shahak wrote, in February 1993, *"Since the spring of 1992 public opinion in Israel is being prepared for the prospect of a war with Iran, to be fought to bring about Iran's total military and political defeat. In one version, Israel would attack Iran alone; in another it would "persuade" the West to do the job. The indoctrination campaign to this effect is gaining in intensity. It is accompanied by what could be called semi-official horror scenarios purporting to detail what Iran could do to Israel and the West and the entire world when it acquires nuclear weapons as it is expected to a few years hence.*" Two decades have passed since these words were written. Iran has attacked nobody and developed no nuclear weapons. Yet the propaganda juggernaut rumbles on.

Of course, Israel justifies all of its actions that meet with international criticism (and there are enough of them, judging from the number of United Nations resolutions it has ignored and/or contravened over the years) by claiming they are necessary to its security. It has never hesitated to describe the stateless, powerless, impoverished Palestinians as a threat to its very existence, despite itself being a nuclear power and one with the unparalleled support of a country which continues to arm and fund it to the tune of $3 billion per annum. It continues to use the most advanced military hardware against defenceless civilians, seemingly oblivious to the fact that, since its very inception, Israel has done most of the killing and Palestinians have done most of the dying. Israel continues to bemoan the absence of worthy leaders of the Palestinian cause while doing its best to assassinate them (although "targeted killing" is the preferred term). It has not hesitated to destroy Palestinian educational establishments and then question why the Palestinians cannot boast an educated class like the Israelis. In short, Israel does everything in its power to depict Palestinians as a non-people, undeserving of the dignity and rights that the rest of the civilised world takes for granted.

In tandem with its military activity, Israel's public relations onslaught ensures that criticism is kept to a minimum and/or ruthlessly countered. The Palestinians are always shown to be the warmongers and obstructers of peace

– but even intellectuals from a Jewish background, such as Noam Chomsky, have spent decades detailing Palestinian peace initiatives which have been scuppered by Israel. And now that it is becoming more and more difficult for Israel to conceal its crimes, and thereby maintain its mythical status as the powerless lamb about to be devoured by Arab wolves, its actions are becoming increasingly desperate. The 2006 invasion of Lebanon drew widespread international condemnation, which had absolutely no effect on the Israeli government whatsoever. Only two countries steadfastly refused to call for an immediate ceasefire: the United States and the United Kingdom. This served to reinforce the belief of many Muslims that Israel is nothing more than an imperialist colonising venture.

The impression that emerges after a cursory glance at the history of Western involvement in Muslim countries, for many Muslims at least, is that double standards prevail. Democracy is the ideal to be pursued unless the "wrong" people win the elections. To this day, Israel and the United States refuse to recognise the legitimacy of the Hamas electoral victory in Gaza, insisting that they never support "terrorists" – ignoring, of course, the occasions when they do. Israel's own "terrorists", such as Menachem Begin and Yitzhak Shamir, were rewarded with becoming the prime ministers of that country. Ariel Sharon is another who was able to operate with impunity, despite his decades-long history of anti-Arab violence, his most infamous involvement being in the Sabra and Shatila massacres in Lebanon. Yet Israel and its leaders have consistently enjoyed the unflinching support of the United States. Not only do they provide Israel with money, weapons and technology, but they also regularly safeguard Israel from reproach by the rest of the world – at least, insofar as the rest of the world is represented by the United Nations.

Israel has no questions asked of its nuclear programme, and is not a signatory to the Nuclear Non-Proliferation Treaty. According to Israel Shahak in his book *Open Secrets, Israeli Nuclear and Foreign Policies*, "The development of Israeli nuclear power is financed by the US. Money for this purpose can be obtained only if Congress toes the line of the organized segment of the American Jewish community and of its various allies. And in the process, the American public must be effectively deceived about Israel's strategic aims." Contrast that to the incessant threats aimed at Iran, which has not only signed the Treaty but also does not possess Israel's violent antecedent history. Again and again, we can see blatant inconsistencies in Western responses to breaches of United Nations resolutions. Iraq was decimated, ostensibly for failing to abide by such resolutions, and thereby indicating its scorn for "world opinion"; Israel's consistent disregard for the same institution, however, results in no sanction whatsoever. It has had more UN resolutions made against it than all other countries combined, but will never be called to account, because of the protection of the United States.

It is not just when considering Israel that these double standards are apparent. India and Pakistan are two other interesting cases in point. They are both nuclear powers, but their treatment by the West differs greatly. In more recent times, India has begun to exert its economic muscle and is, therefore, understandably courted by the likes of the UK and the US. It was not always thus, however, and yet throughout this period there was a difference in treatment that many Muslims regard as dating back to the days of Empire. Jinnah, the founder of Pakistan, was regarded as the troublemaker for his insistence on the rights of the Muslim minorities, whereas the wily Nehru was regarded much more as "someone we can work with". This perceived bias was viewed as the reason that, at the time of partition, various Muslim majority areas did not go to Pakistan when, in fact, they should have done under the relevant agreements. The fledgling state almost emerged stillborn, as it was also deprived of finance and armaments that again were due to it. Those who regard this as an example of anti-Muslim bias point to the on-going issue of Kashmir as evidence. They highlight the fraud by which India sent troops to Kashmir in 1947 as the catalyst for what followed, and observe that despite the United Nations calling for a plebiscite in 1948, this has never taken place. Since then, the West has called for the independence of other areas such as East Timor (where the occupied are non-Muslim, but the occupiers are Muslim), but failed to put pressure on India, despite the fact that the Kashmir dispute continues to destabilise the area.

There is no doubting India's economic power today, and that power is reflected in the West's attitude towards it. For decades, however, India's sympathies lay with the Communist Soviet Union rather than the United States. It was Pakistan which was pro-American, Pakistan which supported the Afghan Mujahideen against Russia on America's behalf, Pakistan which sustained the exodus of Afghans fleeing that war, Pakistan which had to deal with the influx of American weaponry destined for that war, and

Pakistan which is still paying the price and suffering the effects of increased extremism – a by-product of that war, which had played only a marginal role in Pakistani society before then. Since then, despite the fact that both countries received censure for their nuclear tests in 1998 (when Pakistan responded to India's tests with a display of its own nuclear muscle), India has been rewarded with a deal for nuclear assistance from the US, while Pakistan's nuclear programme is viewed with some consternation in the West. This may be understandable, but it fails to take into account that Pakistan is dwarfed by a bigger, more powerful, more prosperous neighbour, which in some quarters still resents its very creation.

❧ ❧ ❧

Sadly, although Muslims may be justified in pointing out the existence of such double standards in the West's dealing with the Islamic world, they fall into error when they allow this to preclude any proper introspection and self-criticism. It can also lead them to adopt a selective reading of history. Just as many who are ill-disposed towards Islam and Muslims choose to focus only on negative examples from the past and present, so, too, do some Muslims ignore aspects of history that do not fit their "West against Islam" thesis. They readily invoke the Crusades, but forget that, prior to that chapter in history, there were significant episodes of mutual trade and interaction which were not based on hatred. The history of Muslim Spain is a fascinating example of relatively positive relationships between Muslims, Christians and Jews which contributed to the creation of tolerant, thriving cities such as Cordoba. This period came to an end with the Reconquista, but focussing on that, while ignoring the previous 800 years, would do a grave injustice to the historical facts. And, even at the time of the Crusades, there was a distinction between the Eastern Christians who had learned to live in harmony with others, and their Latin counterparts who clearly had conquest on their minds. Such examples illustrate the dangers of adopting an absolutist approach that relegates great swathes of humanity into one or other supposedly opposing camp.

There is much condemnation by Muslims of the West's military interference in their countries. As we have seen, intervention can take many forms, from the military and technological support of unsavoury regimes, to the direct military action in Iraq and Afghanistan. Condemnation is often justified, but should not obscure, firstly, other facts of history, and, secondly, military misdeeds committed by Muslims themselves. It can hardly be the Muslim position that we object to non-Muslims exterminating Muslims because we reserve that right to ourselves. There are countless examples of Muslims being killed by Muslims. Some of the most brutal treatment of Palestinians has been at the hands of fellow Muslims. Up to a million people died in the Iran-Iraq war, and perhaps a similar amount in the conflict between West and East Pakistan, which led to the birth of Bangladesh. The Kurds have been oppressed by several Muslim states, while civil war has been a regular feature of certain states in Africa. None of this makes for happy reading, and cannot all be blamed on the interference of the West. It may well be the case that the seeds of certain conflicts were sown by colonisation, but, although the "coloniser" may have a lot to answer for, questions should also be asked of those who allow themselves to become "colonisable".

The reasons for the weakness of certain Muslim countries is a topic upon which many books can and ought to be written. Suffice it to say that we have to get our own house in order first. Yes, Muslims are entitled to, and should, criticise interference by foreign powers in the affairs of Muslim countries, but such interventions are not new. Many Muslims are understandably heartbroken at the devastation wrought, predominantly by America, in Iraq, but even this is not a new phenomenon. When the Mongols invaded Baghdad in the 13th century, they were just as destructive, but the fact remains that today their descendants are hardly known, whereas Islam and its followers are still a significant presence on the world stage. Muslims should be aware that the idea of one community being "checked" by means of another is referred to in the Quran itself, where God indicates that societies do get replaced by others, and that this is all part of God's plan – particularly when those societies have abandoned the standards by which they ought to live. First and foremost, being a Muslim should mean living according to certain principles, whether individually or collectively. If they fail in this regard, then they need to recall that Islam is not the property of Arabs, or any other race, and, as per the Quranic warning, if they do not live their Islam the way they should then they will be replaced by those who do.

In attempting to answer questions about the weaknesses of Islamic states, one inevitably has to consider the technical deficiencies of certain Muslim countries which enabled them to be colonised so readily. There were also serious inadequacies in their political organisation, insofar as they *were* organised, which also played a part in their downfall. Even today, we see few examples of Muslim countries with a laudable degree of popular participation in the governing of the country, or countries where the level of education is to be envied. As long as politicians in certain Muslim countries think that, as their own children will be educated in the West, educating the rest of the nation will only cause them, the leaders, problems in the future, then there is little hope.

There may well be good reasons to resist an American-style democracy, where raising of huge amounts of money is crucial, and which is, therefore, a recipe for corruption. But the despotism that is so often the default position in Muslim states is hardly a worthy alternative. In fact, many Muslims rightly argue that government by "mutual consultation" is a Quranic injunction rather than a mimicking of the West. They suggest that human rights, rather than being a Western invention, actually form the bedrock of Islamic society. Yet who would believe this after considering many contemporary Muslim societies, which seem oblivious to the very concept?

Somewhat belatedly, perhaps, the focus of the anger in parts of the Middle East is shifting from Israel to the deficiencies of their own governments. The issue of Israel's treatment of the Palestinians remains as important as ever, but there is little disputing the fact that many an Arab regime has used it in the past to deflect criticism of its own shortcomings. As long as it could portray Israel as the source of all the Middle East's problems, those advocating domestic reform were never likely to gain much ground. And, more often than not, although there was apparent official enmity directed towards Israel in order to satisfy the domestic population, that did not preclude deals being done at state level between these most intractable of foes. The events of early 2011 illustrated, however, that there was an appetite for change amongst the populations of these Arab countries, and that they did not perceive Israel as the source of all their problems. Similarly, the protests were not led or organised by so-called Islamists, and few, if any, were seeking refuge behind simplistic slogans like "Islam is the solution". It may be that at the time of writing there is a genuine new dawn for those in the Arab world, and that it may herald the start of a new era of useful contribution to the world.

For such a contribution to be authentic, it cannot be beholden to Western concerns. In the early stages of the Arab uprisings in early 2011, there was much discussion in the Western media of Islamism filling the void if the despots were to be removed. This took little account of the reality that Islamic extremism played little or no part in the anti-government demonstrations. Just as this detail appeared to have been missed, or ignored, so, too, was the fact that, although the demonstrations were not "religious" as such, the protesters were not denying their Muslim identity. They were Muslims, they worshipped the One God and were going to continue to practise Islam. It was just that they wanted a say in the way they were governed, and that did not mean they wanted secular tyrannies to be replaced by religious ones. This possibility seemed to be totally lost on many Western commentators who could not see that perhaps there was an alternative model which could include religious faith without that meaning rule by clerics.

Contemporary Muslims were showing that they were still angry. Now, however, they were making it clear that their anger was not some randomly directed impotent rage reflecting their stagnation. Rather, it was focussed, considered and fully alive to the opportunities that the modern world had to offer. They wanted to play an active role in that modern world, and they wanted to play it while remaining committed to their faith.

6

So who is the enemy?

I have many fond memories of the 1980s, but one of the more disconcerting images I recall is of the then prime minister, Margaret Thatcher, announcing on television, after the fall of the Berlin Wall, that, following the defeat of Communism, the next enemy was militant Islam. Excuse me? Militant Muslims may well have been a source of irritation for some at the time, but surely little more; they could hardly be such threatening enemies that it was appropriate to mention them in the same breath as the Communists who had troubled the Western world for the best part of half a century. In fact, hadn't some of those Islamists – the Mujahideen, who were so lauded by the Western media – just defeated those Communists in Afghanistan? Yes, the very people who later brought you Mullah Omar and his not-so-happy band of Taliban had heroically seen off the might of the "Evil Empire", and had been funded and armed by the forces of freedom. Yet here was one of the leaders of that free world teeing up the aforementioned freedom fighters as the next global enemy. Global conflict, the public were being told, was not a thing of the past.

It might have seemed somewhat incongruous at the time, but it was entirely in keeping with the way many Muslims believed the West to be operating. This is perhaps best illustrated by what happened in America immediately after the defeat of Communism. Having finally won the Cold War, and lost many lives in the process (not only in Vietnam, but elsewhere), having conducted wars by proxy across the globe, wreaking havoc in the process, and having expended billions of dollars in countering anything vaguely resembling a Communist threat, both at home and abroad, one might think that the United States of America might reduce its defence budget – at least while it gave peace a chance. Not so. The fact that the defence budget immediately *increased* emphasizes how the USA was being governed: by huge business interests, for huge business interests. It also led many to question whether Communism really was the threat to our individual freedoms it had been depicted to be, or whether it was more a threat to a system which pandered to the rich and powerful.

The real "threat" was that posed by any system seeming to present an alternative way of life to the Western model of unchecked capitalism, which so enriched a tiny minority at the expense of the majority. Fortunately for the West, the major alternative – Communism – was seriously flawed and, therefore, deeply unattractive to the populations of countries which were understandably proud of their post-war success and liberal freedoms. The images of repression emanating from the Soviet Union made it easier to convince people that this was a way of life which needed to be resisted – particularly as the atheist forces of Communism denied the existence of a God who was a very real presence in many Americans' lives.

But it is by looking at their dealings with other parts of the world that we can see the intentions of the West – particularly the USA – in a clearer light. For it was not the godless Communism that was being "resisted", but any socially progressive initiative whose aim was to support the poor majority at the expense of the rich minority – particularly if there was a danger it could set an example to others who may have wanted to follow suit. One does not have to look far to find cases in point. The history of US involvement in Latin America is replete with examples of American efforts to undermine genuine democracies which did not serve the interests of wealthy elites (these efforts were, of course, always clothed in the garb of fighting Communism). And it was not so much that the wealthy elites were valuable in themselves, their main value lay in their support of the capitalist system. Chile had enjoyed over forty years of uninterrupted democracy before the election in 1970 of Salvador Allende, a socialist president committed to such unreasonable initiatives as the nationali-sation of large industries and government control of health-care and education. Clearly, this was intolerable. Thus the leader of the free world, Richard Nixon, along with his able lieutenant Henry Kissinger, made it his mission to rid Chile of its democratically elected leader (the euphemism "regime change" is now used for such actions), with the purpose of protecting the interests of big multinationals rather than the people of Chile. The CIA was set to work, doing what it did best – undermining foreign governments and creating instability where none previously existed – and, by 1973, an American-backed military coup, led by General Augusto

Pinochet, had overthrown Allende and embarked on an economic programme more in keeping with the demands of Washington than the needs of Chile.

Chile, however, is not an isolated example of American business interests using their lobbying power to influence US foreign policy. A country such as Guatemala may seem relatively insignificant on the global stage, but its recent history provides a valuable insight into how so-called economic freedom is put into practice, US-style. The political landscape of Guatemala in the early 20th century was dominated by military dictators, which the USA saw no problem with – even if they were openly fascist, as in the case of one General Jorge Ubico – as long as their policies of granting tax exemptions to American corporations, privatising publicly owned utilities, and giving away large tracts of lands remained unimpeded. Inevitably, however, grass-roots opposition to such rule grew in Guatemala, and, in the 1940s – following the October Revolution – a democratically elected leadership took over. Modest social reforms were implemented which, once again, displeased the USA. American corporations, the United Fruit Company in particular, felt that their interests were being undermined, and apparently saw no problem with the methods they had employed to secure disproportionate land holdings.

The election of Jacobo Arbenz in 1951 was due in no small part to his promise of agrarian land reform – undoubtedly good for the people of Guatemala, but less so for the likes of United Fruit. The fact that only two per cent of the population owned 70 per cent of the land led the Arbenz administration to enact a law which meant that local agrarian councils could expropriate, and reallocate, uncultivated land that formed part of huge estates, while paying compensation to the landowners. As most of United Fruit's land was uncultivated, it had a lot to lose. So much so, in fact, that it redoubled its lobbying efforts in Washington to persuade the USA that Guatemala was a Soviet outpost and Arbenz a Communist (ignoring that in his inaugural speech he had promised to make Guatemala a modern capitalist country). What followed was a US-backed military coup by forces whom the CIA had trained, the toppling and subsequent exile of Arbenz, and business as usual for United Fruit.

Most of this chapter, indeed this book, could be spent detailing examples of American efforts to safeguard their business interests in Latin America at the expense of democracy, fairness, and the lives of indigenous peoples (Cuba is perhaps the most infamous example – particularly the, again CIA-backed, Bay of Pigs fiasco). Indeed it would be easier to list the countries in that part of the world which have remained *un*touched by Washington's interference. Wherever there were leftist movements seeking social and economic reform that adversely affected big business, the USA was on hand to undermine them. In Nicaragua, for example, once the CIA-backed dictator Somoza had fallen, the left-wing Sandinistas took over the government. Rebel groups known as the Contras waged a guerrilla war against the Sandinistas, and it was only later revealed that they were supplied illegal arms by the CIA during Ronald Reagan's presidency. Or, in El Salvador, Archbishop Oscar Romero was one of a growing group of priests who were beginning to voice their beliefs that the poor and downtrodden should seek justice in this world, not the next, and pleaded with the US not to assist El Salvador's military regime, which had been carrying out atrocities against its own people. That was enough to get him assassinated; again, the odour of CIA involvement has never fully left the incident, which became the catalyst for the long and gruesome civil war that is estimated to have accounted for over 60,000 deaths.

In the Dominican Republic, the democratically elected Juan Bosch was overthrown by a CIA-backed military coup, and replaced with a right-wing military junta. Similar events in the 1960s replaced Joao Goulart in Brazil, whose heinous crimes included passing a law limiting the amount of profits multinationals could transfer out of the country, nationalising a subsidiary of ITT, and generally promoting economic and social reform. In Ecuador in 1963, President Carlos Julio Arosemena Monroy was overthrown by a military junta after he had criticised the USA and confirmed his support for Cuba.

The pattern kept recurring: any leader or regime which prioritised the welfare of its people over that of American business interests was swiftly, and often bloodily, overthrown. Such regimes were usually leftist in their outlook, which meant that it was, more often than not, right-wing organisations that attracted American support. Although the aforementioned are merely examples from Central and South America, this should not give the impression that such efforts to "support" American business were restricted to this area of the world. The reality, sadly, was quite different. Even a cursory glance at world events over the last 100 years shows how many regimes have been installed and/or removed at the behest of American business interests. The Western reliance upon oil has led to some particularly disagreeable characters being supported around the world, and, although they have occasionally been removed (perhaps "abandoned" is a better description of their demise), it has never happened while they were "on side". From the Shah of Iran to Saddam Hussein, many a despot has been tolerated as long as he fulfilled his obligations to America. Democratically elected leaders, however – from Mossadeq in Iran, Sukarno in Indonesia, right through to Chavez more recently in Venezuela – have been consistently undermined by the world's number one democracy if they dared to have an economic outlook that prioritised anything other than American interests.

The key to understanding this American antagonism is to appreciate that it is not dependent on the colour or creed of the "enemy", but the stance that the enemy has taken towards the way the world economy works. That the West and its institutions should lead it is just one of the assumptions upon which that economy is based. Its true leader should be America, thus American interests have priority over those of any other country. Nobody could possibly dispute that such an economy should be based on capitalist principles, or that the market (obviously "free") is the proper and just arbiter of the spread of wealth. Any leader or regime daring to question such assumptions must be Communist or warped or somehow dysfunctional and, therefore, resisted if the world is to remain free from tyranny.

Once Communism had been replaced by a new enemy, Islam, and the previously anti-Communist propaganda machine had started directing its fire at Islam, many Muslims took the view that perhaps it was not the number of times they prayed that was provoking the wrath of the West, but the fact that their faith may have something to say about how the world economy should operate, and for whose interests.

They began to wonder whether Islam could offer an alternative to the way the world was presently being run, and whether that alternative would be an improvement or not. What was certain was that Islam had in its past run a significant portion of the world, and that the countries within its rule appeared to fare quite well. From Spain in the West, to India in the East, Islam attracted converts quickly. It did not seek to keep religion private, but, rather, wanted its principles to permeate the very running of society. That society was not without its wealthy people, but they, too, were subject to the rules of the faith, and thus had obligations to those less well off, which meant that the gap between rich and poor was never as vast as the one the modern form of capitalism has created. The Holy Book of the Muslims is certainly not silent on economic issues, and the distribution of wealth was a matter of utmost concern to the faithful. Was it possible that it was these features of the religion which made it look like a threat to the economic status quo, and, therefore, to the ruling elites of the modern world?

If the above perusal of various Latin American examples is accurate, then it shows that those holding the reins of global power would strive ceaselessly to undermine any alternative socio-economic model before it could establish itself and begin to set a good example to others. Muslim countries were hardly setting anything vaguely resembling a good example, but why take the risk of that occurring in the future? Happily for the champions of unfettered capitalism, many Muslim countries were poor, backward and poorly governed by stereotypically unattractive dictators straight out of Hollywood B movies. The task of dismissing such countries was, therefore, much easier, but there was always the danger that they may not remain so inherently weak. And, if they ever did get their act together, it would be under the banner of a religion which demanded social and economic justice, outlawed usury, and imposed obligations on the rich and powerful. All of this was potentially troublesome, and necessitated action on many fronts, not least of which was the constant undermining of the faith of the Muslims. A barrage of criticism had to be levelled at Islam to ensure that it never looked like an alternative to anyone seeking another way of organising society.

And what about the Muslims who believe that Western society actually needs some kind of alternative approach? Are they not just basing their views on their own unrealistic utopian vision of a world dominated by Islam? Far from identifying any inherent flaws in capitalism – a system they are more than happy to adopt – don't they just want to have some outward manifestations of Islam, and in the process make everybody else's life much more difficult? They are simply bitter about their own powerlessness and, for that reason alone, seek to provide an alternative to a system that does not need one. They are paranoid in the extreme, and see conspiracies where none exist. Rather than simply accepting that Western actions against certain Muslims are needed to keep the rest of the world safe, they constantly agitate against that very same West which provides them with homes.

Before we can address these questions, we need to ponder the current state of the West, and ask if all is well, or if there are actually serious socio-economic problems that are indicative of an unhealthy society. Is there inequality on an unprecedented scale? Has rampant consumerism degraded our planet to such an extent that our future is at stake? Is the increasing stress we are contending with, both collectively and individually, cancelling out the advantages of our greater economic wealth? Despite that wealth, are we, in fact, less content? And is our physical and mental health, therefore, suffering, even though the material advances of the last few centuries could reasonably have been expected to guarantee our improved well-being? Are we all – from individual families right through to society at large – broken? And if the answer to all these questions is yes, does it not suggest a civilisation which has peaked and which, in the future, will end up playing second fiddle to a strident East? To answer such questions honestly and frankly, one has to consider the ideals and policies of the Western world, which have been starkly brought to our attention over the course of the global economic crisis, to gauge whether or not there are inherent flaws in the system which might make finding an alternative an altogether more pressing concern.

It should be noted that critics of the Western-style capitalism that has brought much of the developed world to its knees are not primarily from the Muslim world. Many an observer has now concluded that the economic convulsions that have wrecked Western economies are an inevitable outcome of the shakiness of the foundations upon which such economies are based. Economies which purport to be value-free – in the sense that they simply let the markets prevail – are actually heavily laden with values, just not those of the general populace, nor those we expect. Socialism does exist, but only for the rich; capitalism is reserved for the poor. The whole system appears to have been established to serve the interests of the rich and powerful at the expense of the powerless majority. Debt, both public and private, has reached astronomical levels, and it is now conceded that future generations are likely to be less well off than we are. Advanced societies, which thought they had moved on from hardship and want, now see a proliferation of the number of food banks, but are forced to adopt ever-harsher measures in order to placate those who hold the debt. How did we get here? What makes this economic system work? What are the causes of its failure and what, if anything, can be done about it?

The purpose of a nation's economy should surely be to serve the general population. Not to serve it in the sense of providing it with handouts, but to serve it by creating circumstances which allow individuals to thrive on different levels. Man is not simply an economic unit, as some would have us believe. There is more to being human than being a cog in a money-making machine. Scientific wonder, artistic genius, emotional connections all serve to remind us how much more there is to life than simply being able to generate and spend money. A nation's institutions should reflect this truth, and work towards achieving what has often been termed the "greater good", and is often erroneously taken to mean the greater economic good. Inevitably, it will have an economic aspect, but not to the exclusion of other goals and aspirations – and certainly not for the enrichment of a tiny minority at the expense of the majority. Yes, society should cater for the entrepreneurial spirit, without which nations can wither. But it should prioritise the creation of the stability and security that such entrepreneurs need in order to succeed. Do present day Western economies help create such conditions, or have they been instrumental in putting us in a worse position now than we were in half a century ago?

When one looks at our modern capitalist economy, one is met with an unedifying sight. It is little exaggeration to say that the City has become a glorified casino. Gambling, or speculation as it is known on the money markets, has replaced any meaningful and constructive activity: speculative transactions now account for over 95 per cent of global daily turnover. Money creation is no longer the job of governments, but of private institutions, and very few of us seem to realise the dangers inherent in this shift, nor the inevitable conflict between the well-being of society as a whole and the need to maximise profits. Even the way this money is created – literally by pressing a key on a computer – has led very few people to question why such "fake" money has to be repaid by "real" money, given that it is loaned out by the very same private banks who created it. These pages will, of course, reveal that I am no economist, but even my simple thought processes can understand the simple obligation of having to repay money borrowed. And yet it is hardly the case that the banks take a chunk out of their profits and say, "This is our money which we are going to lend to you, so it will need to be paid back." If they did, then clearly one could see the moral and legal case for repaying that debt. But, no, they simply "create" money out of thin air, which appears as figures in my bank account, but then has to be repaid by real money earned by me. And as Tarek El Diwany astutely asks, why does the state borrow "manufactured" money at interest from banks, when it could simply and legally manufacture it itself, interest-free?

On the subject of money creation, Abraham Lincoln had this to say, in a Senate document dated to the 23rd December 1865:

> The government should create, issue and circulate all the currency and credit needed to satisfy the spending power of the government and the buying power of the consumers. The privilege of creating and issuing money is not only the supreme prerogative of government, but it is the government's greatest creative opportunity. By the adoption of these principles, the long-felt want for a uniform medium will be satisfied. The taxpayers will be saved immense sums of interest, discounts and exchanges... money will cease to be the master and become the servant of humanity. Democracy will rise superior to the money power.

Here, we begin to get some insight into the causes of the problem. When loans of this manufactured money come to be repaid, they invariably have to be repaid with interest. No wonder the banks are happy. Fake money is created at no cost, but is repaid with real money, plus a percentage. It is a Mafia-esque racket which ensures that the banks cannot lose, and a situation which is brazenly and immorally justified by the disingenuous mantra that we need to repay what we owe. Except, we end up paying a lot more than we owe (assuming we even "owed" it in the first place). This simple system is clothed in convoluted terminology, by those who peddle it, in an effort to lend it an air of respectability. But let us call it by its name: usury. Usury is an economic device prohibited by the world's major faiths – and not without good reason, one may think. Not only does it enslave the individual, but entire nations are beholden to it. And because the amounts owed keep increasing, not only will they never be repaid, but the cost of even attempting to do so becomes astronomic. The relentless economic growth which is required simply to make the interest repayments is, too, colossal. There is an inevitable negative effect on the environment, which is further plundered in the pursuit of the necessary profit, and, ultimately, on the communities and individuals who see their lives become worthless during this exercise in tail-chasing.

Public spending is blamed for the economic mess that we are in, so it is public spending that has to be cut, regardless of the fact that it was the reckless gambling and sheer greed of the money men which caused the crisis. Yet, the fact remains that if the public debt had not been borrowed from private institutions at interest, the consequences of the debt would not have been as severe as they have. Compound interest repayments translate into the following shocking statistics: in 2011, the US federal government paid $454 billion in interest on the federal debt – some 41 per cent of the total $1,100 billion paid in personal income taxes that year. (In the UK for the same period, interest payments amounted to some £50 billion, with tax revenue estimated to be about £570 billion).

Compound interest in the banking sector increases exponentially. On a graph, its curve begins shallowly, but develops into an almost vertical line, which, by its very nature, shows that this is an unsustainable system. The figures spiral out of control until the whole system is in danger of collapse.

To answer El Diwany's question: if governments borrowed from their own public banks, not only would much be saved on interest payments, and, therefore, not have to be taken from the public services we all rely upon, but there would also at least be the possibility that the debt might one day be repaid, a scenario which is impossible as it stands.

This debt slavery is not something that is just foisted on the individual. Most of us in the advanced West now readily accept that our lives are not our own – at least, not for the quarter of a century or more for which we sign up to our mortgages. There are those who, perhaps cynically, take the view that this is simply how modern societies keep their populations in check. It is interesting to note, though, that such tactics are not restricted to individuals, but are applied to whole economies. Many a developing world economy has been tethered to the yoke of perpetual debt, leading to a cycle from which it struggles to escape. Yet the very organisations that purport to assist the developing world are, arguably, the ones pushing them further into an indebtedness from which they are unlikely ever to emerge.

The World Bank and International Monetary Fund may sound to us like respectable organisations dedicated to assisting the less fortunate. Yet, that is not how they are often perceived in the countries they attempt to assist. They are seen as oppressive Westerners, reinforcing a system in which debt is used to control others, and money is transferred from public to private hands, from poor countries to rich ones. Bodies such as the World Trade Organisation are seen as responsible for privatising public services such as health, education and water provision, while at the same time safeguarding Western interests – by supporting the extension of patent laws, for example, in ways which disproportionately affect poorer nations.

Terms such as "structural assistance plan" may imply that, with the help of these bodies, economic progress is being made in such countries – that they are being dragged from their antiquated ways into prosperity. But, sadly, these terms often hide a more sinister strategy, which sees public assets being sold off to private organisations, usually the very multinationals prioritising profit over the welfare of the domestic populations of those countries. Loans are deliberately promoted to such countries in the full knowledge that, realistically, they cannot be repaid. Which justifies further economic intervention – the purchase of national assets at fire-sale prices, for example – and saddles future generations with debt. Thereafter, the domestic populations lose more of their jobs and public services as draconian measures are implemented in order to pay just the interest on the debts incurred. Any "aid" sent to such countries in the meantime comes with conditions effectively signing over the struggling country's assets to Western corporations (usually with assistance from members of the domestic elite who can be trusted to ensure that the nation's interest is not the interest being served).

In countries organised around this economic system, only one group wins: the bankers, or financiers. Even Mervyn King stated, in early 2011, that the banks were to blame for the financial crisis, and that he was surprised the public's anger was not greater. His remarks certainly beg the question why there has not been any uproar from the masses. Yet the fact remains that, despite scandal after scandal, revelation after revelation, the bankers still come out on top.

Surely this cannot be down to luck, or the bankers' superior intellect, but is the result of a system geared towards benefiting the wrong section of society.

While the welfare state is being undermined, portrayed as a haven for scroungers and slackers, it is worth reminding ourselves that its critics seem to have no problem creating a welfare state for the rich – for that is what we are left with when states ensure that profits are privatised and losses are nationalised. Terms such as "bailout" seem innocuous enough, but what do they actually mean? When normal businesses struggle, there is no question of any benevolent party bailing them out, yet, despite failure after failure, banks continue to be deemed worthy of such assistance. We are led to believe that there is no alternative – and we shall return to the question of who it is that helps form and disseminate such opinions – but I have yet to hear a satisfactory explanation for why the money used to bail out the banks cannot be used to pay off the deficit.

Despite this socialism-for-the-rich, we are still fed the line about the free market as a level playing field on which nothing but fair competition determines who wins. This myth conveniently ignores the question of how countries such as the USA achieved their pre-eminence in the world of trade in the first place. Was it by free-market rules that they played, or did they take full advantage of protectionist measures to ensure their success? Again, this is selective socialism from the very country in which mere mention of that term is anathema to most. The myth also ignores the role of transnational corporations and the fact that globalisation, which is held up as a unifying force, in fact means that a few hundred corporations control some 65 per cent of international trade, of which 40 per cent occurs between different parts of the same transnational corporation. The extent of their reach in the quest to maximise profits, and their ability to sniff out low tax environments far and wide, are the only things "global" about them: the profits accrue in the same old hands in the same old places.

The market is free, then, except when it is not, such as when the state is subsidising the arms industry. This is an industry heavily dependent on taxpayers' money. International trade rules ordinarily prevent countries from subsidising their domestic industries – which means that, for example, poor Caribbean countries are unable to support their domestic fruit growers. However, by happy coincidence, for the West at least, international trade agreements, and the WTO, specifically exclude the military from the rules governing global trade. What this means is that the countries which make the weapons – usually the rich, developed nations – are able to subsidise their arms industries in a variety of ways, including purchasing weapons cheaply at home instead of in a normal competitive environment with challengers from outside. The poorer, undeveloped nations do not have this option, so have to resort to purchasing their weapons from said countries, yet again transferring wealth from poor to rich. Cynics may suggest this kind of free market explains why major arms manufacturers, such as Boeing, are all too eager to sponsor meetings such as that of the WTO in 1999, and that it is plain for all to see who is in cahoots with whom, and for what purpose.

This is all goes to show how relevant value judgements are in the field of economics. Who is it, for example, that decides which industries ought to be subsidised? Contrary to what free-market proponents would have us believe, it is very hard to sustain the position that the state should not interfere in the workings of the market. Slavery, for example, was a market trading in humans as a commodity, but there came a time when the state felt it needed to legislate to stop this happening. More recently, once it was understood that the harm caused by cigarettes outweighed any potential benefit, the increase in taxes on, and legislation concerning this habit, influenced the way this market developed. Similarly, bearing in mind current concerns over obesity, one can foresee comparable state interventions in relation to unhealthy foods in the future.

In vibrant and robust democracies, one would have thought that the domestic populations, rather than just those who wield significant lobbying power, might want some say in these kinds of issues. They might, for example, prefer it if those industries creating means of death and destruction were taxed more, and that any subsidies be reserved for more constructive industries, industries seeking to promote health and the common good. Sadly, the trend, if anything, is for the contrary to happen; increasingly, decisions are made by non-elected bodies – such as the Disputes Panel in the General Agreement on Trade in Services (GATS) – which conduct closed hearings and which substitute the will and authority of national legislatures.

We cannot underestimate the role of the media in selling this flawed system to the masses. It is ultimately from the media that we learn there is no alternative to bailing out the banks. It is from the media that we learn to look in disgust upon the rioters of 2011, just as we did upon miners in the 1980s. The media acts as the mouthpiece of big business, referring to profits as "jobs", and failing to highlight the above unsavoury facts about how arms industries operate, and exactly what they contribute to the world. Of course, there is the odd piece of investigative journalism, infrequent nowadays, which reveals some snippet of corporate malfeasance, but this is usually portrayed as isolated misconduct rather than as an example of systemic abuse by the rich and powerful. It may be, however, that, somewhat belatedly, people are beginning to make the connections between the rich and powerful and the corporate media. They are two faces of the same enterprise, which explains why the increase in corporate power over the last half century has been accompanied by a necessary increase in corporate image-making, or public relations, or what the rest of us might call propaganda.

That is the current system, then, and what I am trying to explore is the extent to which Islam is "under attack" because it has the potential to, at the very least, challenge – and, if adopted by a significant proportion of the world, overturn – this prevailing order. We barely need reminding that the Islam practised by many people today is not exactly of the "social progression" variety. I have argued elsewhere in this book that much of contemporary Islam needs to engage in some serious rethinking, on many different levels, if it is to be relevant to the progress of civilisation. But, for now, what I want to consider is what, if anything, Islam could *potentially* contribute to the field of economics. Does the Quran restrict itself to the "spiritual", or is it just as keen to address material matters? Is the Quranic prohibition on *ri'ba* or interest, a constructive and viable proposition in the modern world, or simply a commandment that could only operate in more primitive and less sophisticated societies? And as for the recent trend towards "Islamic finance", what exactly does this entail? Is there more to it than just "Islamifying" the labels attached to conventional banking and finance?

Perhaps the first point to bear in mind is that Islam is a way of life, not an economic theory. Whatever it may have to say about economics, therefore, has to be considered as part of a system addressing the concerns of the total human being, and cannot be divorced from its ethical and moral content. To take one example, Islam stipulates that *zakat* should be payable to the needy by all adult Muslims who have the means. This is effectively a tax of 2.5 per cent on assets (personal assets such as food, clothing and shelter are exempt) which have been held continuously for a period of twelve months. As well as promoting a more equitable distribution of wealth, this stipulation encourages a feeling of kinship across society. Also, as it is payable on net wealth, and such assets over time will inevitably diminish in value, it is hoped that it would, therefore, stimulate healthy investment and circulation of money, rather than hoarding. *If* it is practised properly, this one economic stipulation would have beneficial consequences for society as a whole. The caveat is crucial, however, because if one begrudgingly hands over 2.5 per cent of one's wealth, or thrusts a coin into the hand of a beggar while not even affording him a smile, then, although one would be following the *letter* of the law, one would not be following its spirit. In that sense, at least, the action would not be Islamic, and would not lead to the social change envisaged.

So it is that economic prescriptions cannot be divorced

from the ethical and moral framework within which we are expected to operate. Concerns for the environment, for example, are central to Islamic belief: the Quran teaches that all that we have is simply held by us on trust; one day, we will have to account for how we have dealt with it. If, therefore, through sheer greed and wanton consumerism, we set waste to our surroundings, and squander our resources, our behaviour would be counter to Islam, and something for which we would be accountable in the eyes of God, regardless of whether or not we had paid our 2.5 per cent. According to Muslim belief, all humans will one day have to answer to a higher authority for their actions; the knowledge of that day to come should colour everything we do. It is against that backdrop that we should view what Islam has to say about economic matters, and appreciate that its economic solutions, if all its other moral and ethical pronouncements were ignored, would amount to nothing more than putting a plaster on a gaping wound. Let us consider, for a moment, the well-known Islamic economic principle that forbids dealing in *ri'ba*, or interest. The following verses from Surah al-Baqarah (Chapter 2) of the Quran make this clear:

> those who devour usury will not stand except as stands one whom the Evil one by his touch has driven to madness. That is because they say "Trade is like usury", but God has permitted trade and forbidden usury... (2:275)
>
> God will deprive usury of all blessing, but will give increase for deeds of charity... (2:276)
>
> Oh you who believe! Fear God, and give up what

remains of your demand for usury, if you are indeed believers. (2:278)

Although these verses clearly deal with usury, they are put into context by the message of the following verses, which emphasise the ethical rationale and moral underpinnings of such rules:

Those who believe, and do deeds of righteousness, and establish regular prayers and regular charity, will have their reward with their Lord: on them shall be no fear, nor shall they grieve. (2:277)
If the debtor is in a difficulty, grant him time until it is easy for him to repay. But if you remit it by way of charity, that is best for you if only you knew. (2:280)

That Islam has something to say about interest is known. What is less well-known is what other religions have had to say on it. The following Old Testament verses show how the prohibition on usury was also a feature of Judaism:

If thou lend money to any of My people, even to the poor with thee, thou shalt not be to him as a creditor; neither shall ye lay upon him interest. (Exodus: 22:25)
And if thy brother be waxen poor, and his means fail with thee; then thou shalt uphold him: as a stranger and a settler shall he live with thee. Take thou no interest of him or increase; but fear thy God; that thy brother may live with thee. Thou shalt not give him thy money upon interest, nor give him thy victuals for increase. (Leviticus 25:35–37)

He that putteth not out his money to usury, nor taketh reward against the innocent. He that doeth these things shall never be moved. (Psalm 15:5)

He withholds his hand from sin and takes no usury. (Ezekiel 18:17)

In the Christian tradition, no less a figure than St Thomas Aquinas argued that usury ought to be forbidden, as it amounts to charging twice for something, once for the item itself and once for its use. Perhaps it is not surprising that the monotheistic faiths take this position, but the more one looks into history the more one encounters prohibitions on usury spanning the length and breadth of the world. We find it condemned by Aristotle and Plato in ancient Greece, in ancient China as well as Rome, and even early Vedic texts from India and Buddhist scriptures speak against the charging of interest.

Yet the prohibition on usury is not a prohibition on trade, as is categorically stated in the Quran (see 2:275 above). It is a prohibition on a fixed or predetermined rate of return on financial transactions – not the uncertain rate of return, such as that represented by profits. Islam stipulates that in order for the investor to share in the profit he must share the risk: he must be part of the venture. Simply to invest the money and expect it to be returned with an increase, regardless of the success of the venture, would amount to making money simply by having money, not by taking any risk, or by doing any work, or by any effort or sacrifice at all. Making money from money is forbidden in Islam, and has led to the development of Islamic banking, where the bank is effectively in partnership with the debtor. Not unsurprisingly, this encourages banks to actively seek out and invest in worthwhile businesses, as they have a stake in their success. This can only be healthy for an economy, and can only lead to a more even distribution of wealth (and it would, of course, avoid situations such as the recent sub-prime debacle).

Islamic banking has become a $300 billion industry, and is growing year on year. There is still much debate about how truly "Islamic" some of its institutions and their practices are, but they are still in their infancy. Their growth, if nothing else, reflects a desire on the part of the public, and it is noteworthy that it is not just Muslims who seek to invest their money in such institutions. If they were simply called ethical banks, rather than Islamic banks, there would be much less stigma attached to them. Certainly, their principles appear to be shared by others. The JAK Medlemsbank in Sweden, for example, adopts the following principles: charging interest is inimical to a stable economy; interest causes unemployment, inflation, and environmental destruction; interest moves money from the poor to the rich, and favours projects which yield high profits in the short term. Its goal is to abolish interest as an economic instrument, and to replace it with other instruments which are in the people's best interests. Its main aim is to provide its members with viable, feasible financial instruments which are environmentally sustainable and serve the local economy.

❧ ❧ ❧

The image of Muslims as some sort of organised enemy

plotting to take over the world, then, may well be a deliberately concocted façade, designed to obscure the reality, scare the general population, and protect those who act like the true enemy of the people: those who benefit from wars and global instability, those who benefit from arms production and arms sales, those who install and remove regimes to suit their own purposes, and those who help create the cultures in which all this can take place. Those, in other words, who are making the most money out of all this chicanery, and, more often than not, have funded it. They are the ones who economically exploit others. Although they wear smart suits and look civilised, they are responsible for death and destruction on a vast scale. According to UNICEF, 22,000 children die each day due to poverty, yet the world of finance is still loath to change its obscene bonus culture.

Although the economic problems of modern Western societies may be the most pressing ones at the moment, it would be foolish to address them in isolation. They are interwoven with social difficulties. They are interwoven with environmental concerns. Solutions need to be holistic, not just in the way they address the practical difficulties, but also in their appeal to the whole of humanity. Any practical answers need to be part of a moral-ethical framework which endures beyond the immediate period of unease. Any such solutions need to take into account humanity's spiritual as well as its material needs.

7

And who are the silent majority?

Is there such a thing as a normal Muslim? And by "normal" I do not mean "typical" because, after all, there are more than a billion of us around the planet, so it may be difficult to identify what it is that is typical about any of us. It may, therefore, be easier for now to define "normal" in terms of what I do not mean: not violent; not backward; not enslaved to out-dated cultures and traditions; not insistent on oppressing women; not bound to notions of honour which might lead to actions that are contrary to the faith itself; not afraid of, nor hateful towards, those who espouse different beliefs and ways of life; not constantly reminiscing about a bygone age that only exists in our minds; and not averse to using our intellectual capacities to think about how we might create a better future for others as well as ourselves. By "normal", in short, I mean people who have the same desires and goals for their families and communities as the rest of humanity.

There are those who would say that, of course, there are normal Muslims. They would say that such Muslims are the silent majority who quietly go about their business in a law-abiding and civilised fashion. Such Muslims do not attract or provoke negative reactions, either regarding their beliefs or their actions, and they live their lives in harmony with their neighbours. The fact that such people do not get any media attention does not mean they do not exist. By their very nature, they are not likely to seek publicity for what they do, and it is unfair when negative news items relating to Muslims cause others to ask, pointedly, "So where is the silent majority, then?", the implication being that if such a silent majority truly existed, it would be as visible as the extremists whom we see so often and so clearly.

I remember once attending a dinner celebrating the 10th anniversary of a particular firm of solicitors. They happened to be Muslims, and so it was no surprise that many of the guests had a similar background. Most, including those at my table, were well-educated, British-born Muslim professionals. The conversation soon turned to whether Muslims should engage with the media. I suggested it was a good idea, and expected the rest of the table to agree, and to lament the fact that we were not doing enough of it. I was shocked, therefore, to hear them dismiss the notion out of hand. There was a lack of trust in the media which the guy sitting next to me summed up with the line, "A billion of us in the world, and they can't find a positive story?" He had a point.

Now, I have never been comfortable blaming others for the situation that Muslims find themselves in. Undoubtedly, others have often had a part to play, and this cannot be overlooked, but it seems contrary to the very essence of Islam, with its ideas of individual free will and accountability, to place undue emphasis on the roles played by other people.

There are occasions, however, when serious questions do need to be asked about their agenda, especially in relation to the media. I used to tire of hearing Muslims complain about how biased the media was against them. This did not mean I myself had complete trust in the media, far from it; I just did not welcome conspiracy theories about hidden agendas. Too often, they seemed a convenient mask for our own deficiencies. This outlook was brought into sharp relief by a particular incident that followed the publication of the "Danish cartoons".

These cartoons were deemed offensive towards the Prophet Muhammad by some Muslims, and some of the more extremist members of the faith decided they would safeguard the reputation and dignity of the Beloved Prophet by staging a demonstration in which they donned fake suicide bomber vests and held up banners proclaiming death to the usual suspects. The media lapped it up, and there were headlines everywhere about these undeniably fanatical protesters, as well as images of the hideous banners they displayed. This cast Muslims in a particularly negative light, especially as the demonstration was portrayed as significant in number – a gross distortion: in reality, there were less than a hundred protesters.

When this particular news item was being aired, I happened to be at my mother's house. My mother was watching one of the Muslim satellite channels, which was beaming live pictures from Trafalgar Square, London, where another type of demonstration was taking place. Here, tens of thousands of British Muslims packed out the square, and the banners they held aloft read, "Thank you, Britain, for not publishing the cartoons." What would the effect of the Trafalgar Square images have been on the British public? They would probably have been given a valuable, conciliatory and constructive insight into the "silent majority". Sadly, however, these images were nowhere to be seen on mainstream news channels. Nor did they merit any mention, let alone headlines, in the press. Had those images from Trafalgar Square been shown to the general public, they would in all likelihood have had a positive effect on the public's perception of Muslims. By holding them against the backdrop of the peaceful majority, they would have put into perspective the actions of the extremist minority. The fact that the peaceful demonstration took place in the heart of London meant that there was no excuse for not knowing about it. It seems reasonable to assume, therefore, that conscious decisions were made not to show such positive images, and it is appropriate to question why. In not showing such images, any debate about the existence and role of the silent majority of Muslims is prevented from properly taking place; discussion is restricted to the usual topic of extremism. This reinforces the view of many that there is a specific agenda to keep a particular aspect of Islam in the forefront of the public's mind, to the exclusion of other facets of the faith and its followers.

The media's responsibility does need to be highlighted, as it is instrumental in forming opinion about the silent majority. But it has an arguably limited impact on the reality of the group itself. Who are the "normal" Muslims, and what is it that they do? Who speaks for them? Is it enough for Muslims to be normal in the sense of being law-abiding members of society, or should they be doing more? Are there differing strands of thought available to Muslims, or do they belong to a monolithic bloc which allows for no divergence of opinion? Is Islam set in stone, or is there room for debate and dissension?

Most people reasonably conversant with current affairs, regardless of their faith background, are aware of some of the basics of Islamic belief and practice. Most of us are aware that Muslims pray five times a day, fast in the month of Ramadan, and go on pilgrimage to Mecca. These are established duties enjoined upon Muslims. But do Muslims, themselves, reflect upon these practices, or are they simply content to follow the established rituals? Are they even allowed to reflect upon these practices? These are some of the questions I will ask here, and the answers will help us consider whether or not Islam is simply a relic left over from an era of religiosity, or whether it can still have relevance and, perhaps more importantly, any use in the future.

The Quran was revealed at a particular time (the early 7th century) in a particular place (desert Arabia) to a particular people (the Arabs), yet its message is said to be applicable to all of mankind throughout the ages. Can it remain relevant without any human input, or do we have a responsibility to keep it relevant – and if so, how? There are many areas in which this debate could find fertile ground, but the following examples illustrate the point clearly. One of the pillars of Islam is that Muslims should pray the five daily prayers. The times for these are roughly as follows: dawn, midday, mid-afternoon, sunset, late evening. It makes sense to conclude from these timings that they are an attempt to instil in the Muslim (literally, "he or she who submits to God") the desire to remember God constantly, by marking out certain parts of the day as times to put our worldly concerns aside, and put worship first. When we look into the context in which the rules regarding prayer were revealed, we find, unsurprisingly, that Arabia in the 7th century was a society which measured time by reference to the sun. The working day was effectively governed by daylight hours, and the prayer times reflected that.

Things have moved on in the last fifteen centuries or so. Despite the wishes of many people, Muslims are not confined to the Middle East, but now inhabit practically every region of the world, including Scandinavian countries, like Norway, in the northern parts of which there are, in the winter months, days with no daylight at all, and in the summer, days with no darkness. What should Muslims do there? It does not appear attractive or viable either to omit prayers completely, or to pray continuously. Fatawa (legal opinions) from religious "scholars" have emerged permitting Muslims to follow the prayer times of the nearest Muslim country. But these appear arbitrary and inadequate as solutions, and not necessarily in keeping with the spirit of the original requirement to pray. Does Islam really prevent the adoption of an alternative, which is consistent with the spirit of the injunction, and yet practical in its application?

In the United Kingdom, in the winter months the last four daily prayers can be as close as 12 noon, 2pm, 3.40pm, with the final prayer at 5.30pm – hardly the end of the day. Yet the same final prayer ('Isha) can take place as late as 11pm in the summer months. The dawn prayer is at 7am in winter, but a somewhat inconvenient – and, therefore, more readily missable – 3am in summer. Is this what God intended? If the requirement to pray according to the position of the sun is unalterable, then one could argue that it is. If, however, the sun timings were simply revealed because that is how the recipients of the revelation happened to measure time, then it is theoretically possible for alternatives to be made available to the Muslim community. Also, rather than any verse stipulating the inherent holiness of the sun and moon, the Quran actually contains the opposite: there are Quranic verses (such as 6:96) which clarify that the sun and moon are not inherently holy, but relevant only for the purposes of marking time.

Now, in the modern world, very few of us mark time by reference to the sun. The vast majority of the developed world's population tells the time by referring to their watches, not by looking out of the window. Recalling that the purpose of the five daily prayers appears to be marking the day so as to remember our Creator at regular intervals, what is there to prevent us adopting the following timetable in Britain: early morning prayer at 6am, midday prayer at 12noon, afternoon prayer at 4pm, early evening prayer at 7pm and late evening prayer at 10pm? These times could apply throughout the year. A single prayer time could apply throughout the country. The timings would be consistent with the nature of the working day in many modern societies, and, with the increased certainty, employers might well be more amenable to their workers taking time out for their worship. Of course, there would need to be some fine-tuning according to the requirements of different countries, along with in-built flexibility and allowances where exceptions need to be made, but none of this appears to contravene the spirit of the faith. On the contrary, it keeps the faith meaningful and relevant in the 21st century.

It would also have an added advantage for another pillar

of Islam, namely, fasting in the month of Ramadan. The Islamic calendar is based on the lunar year, so Ramadan does not always fall at the same time; it is generally about ten days earlier each year. At present in the United Kingdom, for example, when Ramadan falls in the winter months, the daily fast is roughly from 7am to 4pm. Yet, in the summer months, it can be as long as from 3am to 10pm. Now, let us for a moment consider the purpose of fasting. It is clearly stated in the Quran that fasting is prescribed to us so that we may "learn self-restraint". It is also made clear in the Quran that our Creator does not seek to put us in any "hardship". Going without a spot of lunch in the winter months is, arguably, not going to teach us a great deal of self-restraint. Similarly, going without food and water for up to 19 hours in the summer months, in addition to the loss of sleep involved in getting up for the 3am breakfast and prayers, could arguably be described as hardship, and might just make us feel more tired and irritable, rather than closer to God and spiritual.

Again, it is useful to bear in mind that when God told the Arabs in the 6th century to fast from dawn until dusk, he was giving them a timeframe which was more or less consistent with their working day. As it happens, the position of Arabic countries in relation to the Equator means that the length of the day in the region is roughly the same in winter as it is in summer: around 12 hours. So, God was telling the Arabs to fast for about 12 hours. Such a fast would be entirely feasible if one were to adopt the revised prayer timetable suggested above, starting the fast with the early morning prayer at 6am, and ending it with the early evening prayer at about 7pm. This would not only be consistent with the working day, but would also allow for the reflection and prayer which should be part of Ramadan, but which is a struggle in the summer months, when the night prayers only end shortly before the next fast begins, leaving little time for any reflection or contemplation. Such a schedule would satisfy both our spiritual *and* material needs.

There is yet another "pillar" of Islam which could be reconsidered. (It is understandable, if somewhat unfortunate, that these tenets of the faith are described as "pillars", as it gives the impression that they are intended to be immovable, but the label is a man-made rather than God-given one.) The Hajj, or pilgrimage to Mecca, is a duty that all adult Muslims have to perform at least once in their lifetime. A lesser, voluntary pilgrimage called the Umrah, can be performed at any time of the year, but the Hajj itself must be performed at a particular time. Every year, despite the authorities' best efforts, the sheer logistical nightmare of administering up to two million people in one place can cause all sorts of crowd control problems, and puts the pilgrims in physical danger. Is this what was intended when the Hajj was first made obligatory?

What if all of the world's one billion Muslims were to turn up on the same day to perform their religious duty? They would be attempting to fulfil their religious obligations, but would inevitably be prevented by the authorities from doing so. The safety of the general public would be given priority over religious duties, and accommodations would be made which would be deemed not to contravene the spirit of the religious requirement. Many of the rituals that form part of the Hajj have been similarly modified to meet human needs rather than any perceived Divine ones.

The symbolic stoning of the pillars, which represents the shunning of evil, is now the stoning of large walls with basins underneath to catch the stones and avoid accidents. Routes are made one-way to avoid any trampling tragedies. The sacred Hajr e Aswad, or Black Stone, does not have to be directly touched, but can now merely be pointed towards, such is the sheer volume of people attempting to approach it.

The fact is that such accommodations are already being made in certain areas and can, therefore, at least theoretically, be made in others. It is not difficult, for example, to envisage a time when there are so many Muslims wishing to perform the pilgrimage that it is simply not feasible for it to occur on one day in the year. Could the authorities then be in a position to say that the Muslim population has reached such a size that in future the Umrah will count as the Hajj? If so, it could be spread across the year, taking away the logistical problems and the attendant safety issues. And if, as some suggest, the purpose behind the Hajj is to create a meeting place where Muslim issues and problems can be addressed, a sort of annual conference, then is this not likely to be more useful if it is attended by those who are in positions of authority and leadership? An annual convention where Muslims bring not only their problems and grievances, but also their ideas and solutions, is probably long overdue (and, arguably, some way off, given the current state of the Muslim world), but it is the type of progressive initiative which the community is crying out for.

The point I am making here is that there is scope for religious rituals to be amended to suit changing circumstances, and that such amendments are not contrary to the faith. Innate religious conservatism makes this tweaking of tradition anathema to many followers of the faith, so the impetus for such change cannot come from lay people, but has to come from scholars, thinkers, and those with a measure of authority in Islamic matters. It should also be emphasised that these are ideas held by, or at least articulated by, just a small minority of the Muslim population, but which need to be considered if Islam is to remain relevant to the modern world. It needs to be clarified that they are not contrary to the spirit of Islam, and are only contrary to the letter of the law if one takes a literal approach to it, which not only goes against its spirit, but can also defy common sense. These kind of ideas need to be addressed by the religious authorities of Islam if they want to avoid being marginalised, and their faith becoming a collection of meaningless rituals. It is normal in other faiths to address the question of tradition versus modernity, resistance to change versus progressive evolution of religious practices, and it should become the norm in Islam, too, rather than the preserve of a tiny reform-minded academic elite. These are the topics that Muslims should be discussing over dinner.

So, what is the normal kind of thinking going on in the Muslim world? Is there any thinking going on in the Muslim world? In order to gain some insight into the views of normal Muslims, perhaps the most useful starting point is to listen to some prominent Muslim voices. We are all too familiar with the inflammatory ranting of extremist preachers, but, given their very limited following, they clearly do not represent the majority of the community. There are no significant protests at their detention, and one can well understand that most Muslims would gladly see the back of them so that they can concentrate on their own lives and families. Yet, it is almost as if these preachers have a tacit understanding with the media, which allows them to get the publicity they desire, and the media the stories they want, regardless of what most Muslims may actually want. To be clear, the media have a right, and a duty, to inform the public of the existence of such extremists in our midst who, at the very least, have derogatory things to say about our way of life, and may well impact on our security. Any objection is simply to a disproportionate and distorted representation that neglects the existence of other voices.

It is useful, however, to look at some of the other representatives of the Muslim faith, particularly those prominent in the media. Firstly, we shall consider those who are critical of Islam and Muslims, bearing in mind that such criticism comes in a variety of forms. (It must be conceded that it is not easy to assess just how representative such voices are. Book sales would be somewhat indicative were it not for the fact that they do not necessarily denote approval. And, in any event, the way such publications are marketed has an impact on the sales figures.) Three quite diverse authors who are often held up as powerful critical voices, if only because each comes from a Muslim background, are Ayaan Hirsi Ali, Irshad Manji and Ed Husain.

Perhaps the easiest to deal with is Ali, who sets her stall out clearly. Having been born in Somalia, renounced Islam, and ultimately found love in the arms of an American neo-conservative, she is, unsurprisingly, not the Muslims' first choice when it comes to self-criticism. She was undoubtedly subjected to ill-treatment, in her early life, which the offenders tried to justify in the name of Islam. But the conclusions she draws about the faith, rather than those responsible for the ill-treatment, show a lack of understanding of Islam which detracts from her value as a critic. Being born into a faith does not necessarily confer understanding, although that is not to demean her experiences. Sadly, she has become little more than a neo-con poster girl, content to be the stick with which they can beat Islam.

A more interesting critic is Irshad Manji. Her Canadian background perhaps made escape less of an issue for her than for Ali, but she, too, was subjected to ill-treatment, in her case by a knife-wielding father. Although at first blush one may question the objectivity of any criticism with such a backdrop, her work merits serious consideration. Her background in the media may explain her penchant for shock-jock tactics and these, coupled with her being openly lesbian, will be enough to send many Muslims running. My first reading of her book, *The Trouble with Islam Today*, left me similarly nonplussed. Her tone evinced a barely concealed contempt for Islam and Muslims, and her constant bleating about being on the verge of leaving Islam made me want to shout back, "Just bloody go, will ya? Sort it out with God, because, quite frankly, I can't be a**ed." It was a book I really had to take a deep breath to pick up, rather like tuning in to another depressing episode of *EastEnders*. You knew it was going to stress you out, and life was difficult enough without this self-inflicted dose of further angst, so why put yourself through it? Well, not only did I put myself through it, but after a suitable period of recuperation, I went back for a second dose. The question was whether or not it was just her style I found objectionable, or whether I had issues with the substance of her work.

Manji should undoubtedly be given credit where it is

due. It is difficult to argue with her calls for honesty on the part of Muslims. She is absolutely correct when she asserts that too many Muslims have developed a victim mentality, and are voluntarily keeping themselves in ignorance – faults which they need to get rid of urgently if they are to contribute usefully to the modern world. When she states that certain Arabs have been setting Islam's agenda for too long, she probably has a point worthy of further investigation, too. Her three proposals for progress, namely, "revitalising Muslim economies by engaging the talents of women; second, to give the desert a run for its money by unleashing varied interpretations of Islam; and third, working with the West, not against it", are utterly commendable. But, regrettably, the six-line paragraph which contains these proposals is obscured by the overwhelming weight of negativity, indeed contempt, which she displays towards Islam and Muslims. It was this which stayed with me on the second read, too, even though this time I had some sympathy for her views.

I cannot help thinking that, to a large extent, her attitude is coloured by her personal experiences. (In a sense, I am grateful to her for this because it was recognising this that encouraged me to think that if her negative experiences could inspire her to write about Islam, then so, too, should my positive experiences similarly motivate me.) Not only does her work reveal her family difficulties, but, also, that the environment around her did nothing to draw her towards Islam; in fact, it distanced her further. Many Muslims growing up in the West will feel similarly about their flawed communities. The difficulty is that, as a result, Manji has no love for the Muslim community, and her calls for reform, therefore, sound like those of a condescending outsider rather than a mournful insider. As any parent knows, rebuking and admonishing have their place, but, ultimately, sympathy and mutual understanding are required for true change to take place in the hearts you seek to influence.

Manji insists on drawing conclusions adverse to Muslims, and such is her wilful refusal to acknowledge evidence that may justify a sympathetic conclusion that the prospects of reaching some mutual understanding recede further with every turn of the page. Her description of Islam as a "gift of the Jews" betrays a completely flawed understanding of what Islam means, and where it stands in relation to other faiths. (It does, however, perhaps explain what she later has to say about Israel.) She says that she desires reform, but the very Muslims who might form the vanguard of such reform are alienated further when she insists on showing not the least respect for the Prophet Muhammad, a man they are taught to love. For example, her description of the killing of the men of the Jewish Banu Qurayzah tribe in the seventh century is reduced to a simple command to "kill the Jews", leaving the impression that, as it was ordered by the Prophet Himself, this must be some sort of Muslim duty, and that they were killed simply for being Jews. One would have thought she would have at least considered Karen Armstrong's account, in her biography, *Muhammad*, which puts into context the treatment of convicted traitors in that period – particularly when they brought a community close to extermination – and highlights how the punishment was, in fact, one chosen by an arbitrator nominated by the Qurayzah themselves. Manji is entitled to come to whatever conclusions she thinks appropriate, but to disregard certain arguments because they do not favour her agenda will inevitably lead readers to question her motives.

A similarly fast and loose approach to the facts is evident in her treatment of the Quran. Manji, I believe rightly, criticises those who do not adopt a contextual reading of scripture. Yet she is more than willing herself to pluck verses out of the book that suit the particular point she is attempting to make, without addressing their context, stating that it is unclear which verses were revealed when. Again, that assertion may carry more force if it was based on serious study of the origins of the text. Not once does she admit to the difficulties inherent in analysing a text in translation; without doing so she resembles the Japanese student of English literature who, having read a Japanese translation of Shakespeare, wonders what all the fuss is about. To speculate that "it's conceivable that the compilation of the Quran had to be rushed to meet imperial pressures", might be a weightier proposition if it was not just based on an article in *The Atlantic Monthly*, and took into account the fact that, although the compilation of the written document might have been treated in a particular way, many people had already committed the Quran to memory by that stage.

But perhaps most importantly of all, in this "wake-up call for honesty and change", Manji does not promote, or even include the many modern and educated, reformist and progressive interpreters of the Quran who, unlike her, have bothered to address the original language of the book, yet do not feel the need to question its authenticity – at least, not on spurious bases. Theirs are voices that need to be heard if Islam is to contribute usefully to the world; ignoring them only gives the impression that they do not exist. Abdullah Saeed's *Interpreting the Quran* is an excellent introduction to analysing the Quran, with particular emphasis on reading it contextually, and deserves at least a mention in Manji's work. Tariq Ramadan and Reza Aslan are also notable by their absence. And as for the many eminent female Muslim scholars and interpreters of the Quran – why ignore them? Unless, of course, they may disagree with you? Amina Wadud's seminal work, *Quran and Woman*, sadly finds no place in Manji's rant.

Manji is equally dismissive of Muslim history. For her, the Golden Age seems like it was nothing more than the incubation period for all the ills of the present day Muslim world. Muslims ruled and/or were a significant presence in Spain for some eight centuries, and helped create the flourishing "ornament of the world" that was the city of Cordoba, yet this gets barely a mention. The House of Wisdom established at Baghdad merits only fleeting attention, too, despite the fact that it attracted the greatest minds of the time. The Muslim presence and continued influence in Sicily is now being belatedly recognised as playing an instrumental role in the European Renaissance (see, inter alia, John Hobson's *The Eastern Origins of Western Civilisation*), yet it does not get Manji's juices flowing. Sadly, she can only find "wholesale discrimination" where others find a degree of civilisation unmatched in the rest of the contemporary world. Lest it be thought otherwise, I have argued elsewhere that Muslims cannot rest on the laurels of previous success, but, if Manji is seeking to promote a new climate of thinking amongst Muslims, then surely emphasising, rather than demeaning, the Golden Age of Islamic history is vital.

So far, then, in her "wake-up call", Manji has questioned one of the most fundamental Muslim beliefs – the divine origin of the Quran – without any compelling evidence other than the fact that she struggled to make sense of it all. She goes on to question the very character of the Prophet, again refusing to give Him the benefit of any doubt, when often His worst enemies would struggle to say anything against Him personally. Oh, and then it's Islamic history that gets it in the neck, containing as it does apparently little of use to humanity. Her attack now in full flow, it seems that her inclusion of Israel into the list of complaints about Muslims was intended merely to administer the coup de grâce. Fair enough, she did get a paid trip to the Holy Land, and it would be downright rude to criticise them after their hospitality – particularly as it seems the Palestinians were not as keen to fund such a trip – but there does not seem to be even the semblance of any objectivity about the Israel-Palestine dispute. It may well be right that this should not be the defining issue for Muslims seeking to live their lives in the West in the 21st century, but there should surely be an acknowledgment of its victims. Countless United Nations resolutions against Israel might just indicate what most of the world thinks of this conflict. But Miss Manji's bile-fuelled juggernaut is not for slowing down, let alone stopping.

Ed Husain, on the other hand, finds me even less sympathetic. Ed, Ed, Ed. Why on earth, for a start, would you want to abbreviate Mohamed to Ed? OK, I accept it is your choice, and maybe again your research showed that books by Eds outsell those by Mohameds (at least in the West), but do you not think that many Muslims might be put off by your new *nom de guerre*? After all, you know how sensitive some of "us" are. But I am getting sidetracked; I, for one, am offended less by your choice of name than by what you have to say. *The Islamist* is very readable and it does make some pertinent observations. You will have to forgive me, however, if I don't buy this "inside track to radical Islam" approach which suggests the reader is about to unearth some grave and hidden secrets about the workings of various shady organisations. To be perfectly frank, many of us (and by "us", I mean those who were never extremist nutters in the first place) find that your book simply confirms what we suspected all along: that those who veered towards extremism were those who, like yourself, were "never quite settled", "a loner at school, occasionally bullied and frequently sworn at", "a misfit" with "no white friends" who suddenly "felt very special" when they joined what they thought was this Global Rude-Boy Massive, which was given a righteous air by virtue of its "Islamic" credentials.

I may be being unfair. Like I said, there are some useful observations in your book, and I genuinely hope it has steered some impressionable youngsters like yourself away from radicalisation. On the other hand, however, there are those who feel you are one of those guys who bends which-ever way the wind blows, and the explanation for your "conversion" is simply that anti-radicalisation is flavour of the month (not to mention where the money is). I am not so sure. I do believe that you are genuinely "moderate" now, and have a greater insight into Islam. But, my goodness, it took an inordinately long time for the penny to drop for you. I mean, what on earth were you thinking, a grown man, working in the City, studying at university, realising that your Islamist ways were a mistake, and then after 9/11 asking "how are we going to celebrate?" Really? You were not 16 years old then, and I'm afraid the "hold" you claim Islamism had on you escapes me.

I think a lot of educated Muslims want to believe you, but have serious reservations regarding your credibility. You will be very familiar with the term "sell-out". It is an easy one to hurl in your direction, but there are those who will think you are saying what your paymasters want to hear. Certainly, you make it difficult for those of us who want to defend you. I mean, there are not many Muslim organisations you have spared in your accusations, and surely you want to have as many Muslims as possible on board with your sentiments about "true" Islam, so why seek to alienate those who hold some degree of authority with Muslim communities? That is not to say that such people are above criticism, but surely a more diplomatic approach would be more fruitful? I know your background is one of seeking confrontation, but one of the advantages of growing up is that we can see the futility of tactics that seemed attractive when we were teenagers. The alternative is that, more often than not, people wish to dissociate themselves from you, which is sad because much of what you purport to believe now is what Muslims, in fact, need to think about.

Another example of your diplomatically ham-fisted approach is your Quilliam Foundation, or Quilliam as it is now known, named after the 19th-century English solicitor William Henry Quilliam, who converted to Islam and, having taken the name Abdullah, thereafter headed up a Muslim community which was quite progressive in much of its outlook. What you clearly did not appreciate, or bother to look into, was that in Liverpool, the birthplace of

Quilliam, there was a society called the Abdullah Quilliam Society which, for several years, had been negotiating with the local council to obtain and refurbish the old site of Quilliam's mosque in order to transform it into a modern heritage centre. This would firstly preserve a significant part of British history, a building which many consider to be the first independent mosque in Britain, and secondly, be a base from which to educate people that Islam is not an immigrant religion brought over just by Pakistanis and Arabs – undoubtedly highly pertinent when it comes to pressing issues of social cohesion, as I am sure you would agree. In its efforts, the Abdullah Quilliam Society works in conjunction with, and with the full support of, Quilliam's remaining descendants. Did you bother to ask the family if you could use their name? Did you make contact with the Society and inform them of your intentions? Sadly, you did not, which made the Society's efforts much more difficult, as it had to spend an inordinate amount of time and energy distancing itself from the Quilliam Foundation once you became mired in controversy.

I could go on. Suffice to say that, happily for Muslims, those who advocate fresh and independent thinking in Islam are not restricted to the Manjis and Husains of this world. Insofar as their efforts are sincere, I truly hope they get a reward that is commensurate with the publicity they undoubtedly have received. But there are others out there, who do not attract such publicity, whose efforts are nevertheless noteworthy.

❧ ❧ ❧

Muslims need to rediscover the spirit of constant intellectual renewal that played such a significant role in their history; in recent times, it has become notable by its absence. To some extent, this is understandable, given the upheavals caused by the period of colonisation. But that explanation only goes so far. It can no longer be used now that colonisation has ended, and education and learning are so readily available to much of the world. Having said that, it would be a mistake to suggest that there is little or no thinking going on in the Muslim world. Tariq Ramadan is perhaps the most prominent intellectual to raise issues of reform, but he is not the only one. Reza Aslan is one of the new breed of Muslim hero, fearlessly tackling Islamophobia on the one hand, and outdated rituals on the other, and doing so in a readily understandable Western idiom. Amina Wadud has grappled with the controversial issue of a female interpretation of the Quran, despite being the recipient of opposition from many in the world of traditional Islamic scholarship. Her work, *Inside the Gender Jihad*, addresses the issue of women and reform in Islam, a subject about which one would think there was no mention by any Muslim, let alone by a female scholar of Islam. And Khaled Abou El Fadl brings reason and tolerance to the fore with his extensive knowledge of the Holy Scriptures, as well as Islamic history.

The fact remains that such thinking does not necessarily get the publicity it merits. Even when reform-minded efforts need every ounce of support they can get, we find that opportunities are spurned. One such advocate of reform said the following in his book, *Islam, Liberty and Development*:

The effect of dogma on our society, which has a religious identity, is vast. And its negative effect is greater than secularism because dogmatic believers usually project an aura of religious legitimacy... Centuries of our history have been governed not by the conscientious and thoughtful effort of the people of the land, but by autocratic and whimsical rulers... Freedom of thought, which represents the key condition of being present on the stage of destiny and the main impetus for dynamism and growth in social life, has not been respected in our society... Our temperament has not been trained to be receptive to freedom... In the past half-century, every time the ground has been ripe for us to experience freedom, we have squandered the opportunity. Sometimes such sentiments emerge from directions we least expect.

In this instance, these words were penned by Mohammad Khatami, the president of Iran from 1997–2005.

These are just a few names and positive steps are being made not just by individuals. Countries such as Malaysia and Turkey have long been involved in reformist thought, and Turkey's recent announcement that it is going to undertake a long-term project which aims to reinterpret the scriptures in the light of contemporary knowledge, is welcome, even if long overdue. Their efforts were not ones of political expedience intended to satisfy the West, but were an authentic initiative from within Islam, which involved extensive work by the School of Theology at Ankara University, precisely the kind of focussed and practical scholarship which the Muslim world had been missing for so long. Such efforts are not only necessary, but also give hope that the future for Islam need not be as bleak as many of today's headlines suggest.

8

How is it looking for the future, then?

I grew up on a diet of chips. I do not mean the greasy potato pieces regarded as "traditional" English cuisine, nor am I referring to the potato-based snacks eaten by our American friends but which we, having invented the language, quite properly call crisps. No, I am talking about *CHiPs*, an American TV series about the California Highway Patrol. Its heroes were Jon, a very plain waspish blond American, and his sidekick Ponch, the exotically named and equally exotic looking Frank Poncherello (who, perhaps coincidentally, looked like a Pakistani bloke). They were two motorbike cops who patrolled the Californian highways and saved the day on a regular basis – well, every Saturday at about 5pm on ITV. *ChiPs*, along with *Starsky and Hutch*, *Dukes of Hazzard*, *Knight Rider* and, later, *Miami Vice*, were the shows that provided the heroes for many a kid in the late Seventies and early Eighties, my formative years. And, along with equally glossy soaps such as *Dallas* and *Dynasty*, they provided this youngster with a portal to a world in which everyone was bronzed and beautiful, a glamorous, glossy world which, to a boy born in Burnley, was how heaven might look. Never mind the 70-odd virgins the tabloids thought I was promised, I was just happy with a heaven full of Pamela Ewings and Daisy Dukes.

So why do you need to know this? Because it is an insight into what I found most appealing growing up. To this day, I can clearly recall leaving the cinema with a pal of mine after watching *Beverly Hills Cop* in early 1985, both of us vowing to relocate to California. Needless to say, neither of us did – we are both still in Liverpool – but back then it just did not get any better than the USA.

Hopefully that sets the scene for my criticism of certain aspects of American life – or, more particularly, its foreign policies. Such criticism is not based on the inherent hatred of all things American which is supposedly drilled into Muslim children from an early age, but is the result of years of witnessing certain actions which were worthy of condemnation, and all the more upsetting because they began to dismantle the idealised picture of America that I had grown up with. Of course, it is one thing to see a place on TV and feeling drawn to it, but surely the reality could not be as exciting and attractive. Yet when I paid my first visit to New York in 1990, shortly after graduating, I still found it to be a place that, like many of the products sold on its streets, gave you an incredible buzz, and got you hooked.

(It was also my first trip abroad, and I learned the invaluable lesson that, if you are a dark-skinned chap with a goatee beard, you do not run through an airport in New York. My flight had been delayed considerably, and I was mindful that Andrew, with whom I was going to stay in

New York, had been waiting for some time. So, as soon as I picked up my luggage I began to run (well, jog) towards the exit. Unfortunately, there was a huge queue. Fortunately, however, as I joined the back of it, a helpful looking police officer approached and asked me to accompany him. As he took me towards the front of the queue, I distinctly remember thinking, "Oh man, how cool is this? The guy has seen that I've only got one bag and am in a hurry, and figured there's no point in me wasting time in the queue, so he's helping me bypass it. Only in America!" Imagine my surprise, then, when he then took me to one side and asked me to open my case. Fortunately, he only found clean underwear, and other accoutrements of the first-time traveller. Unfortunately, however, that did not allay his suspicions, and he went off and returned with a tiny screwdriver with which he began to prod the case in search of a secret compartment. It was at that point that I remembered that the suitcase belonged to my grandfather, and that he had brought it from Pakistan, so for all I knew it may well have had a bloody secret compartment! Just as I began to contemplate life in a small cell with a big man, the officer begrudgingly sent me on my way.)

To this day, my criticism of America is equalled by my admiration for and attraction to it. Now that I am grown up and happily married, I obviously spend less time thinking about Daisy Duke or her modern equivalents, but I am still impressed with American achievements, particularly in film and music. That is not intended to be some sort of backhanded compliment; I can readily accept that, over the years, there have been a few American achievements in areas other than entertainment. I am firmly of the view, however, that some of America's creative output is second to none, and can provide an unexpectedly thoughtful analysis of modern society, whether that be at home or abroad. Films like *Syriana*, *Body of Lies*, *Lions for Lambs* and *Rendition* are admirable for their willingness to explore themes that may be uncomfortable for those who regard American conduct to be unimpeachable. TV series such as *The West Wing* are not just products of genius written by people at the very top of their game, but also provide a commentary on both what America is, and what it could be. (How many of us have secretly wished that the president of the USA really was Jed Bartlet, or even Martin Sheen – which isn't such a far-fetched idea, seeing as acting seems to be a necessary skill in that particular office?)

Perhaps this discussion of American entertainment does nothing more than highlight one important fact. I am not, nor do I want those around me to be, interested in holding one-dimensional views when approaching world affairs. America is neither simply good nor evil, and although much is made of it being regarded as the "Great Satan" by certain sections of the Muslim world, so, too, do Muslims suffer from being poorly and prejudicially regarded by sections of the Western world. America should certainly be taken to task for its misdeeds, and perhaps it can be argued that of those to whom much is granted much will be expected. This places on America's shoulders a greater responsibility to ensure that its stability and prosperity are used for the greater good rather than merely to enforce its own interests around the world. This may be a utopian ideal, but if we are to progress beyond our current materialist obsessions, then someone somewhere is going to have to take the lead. At the same time, just because I may on occasion be critical of America, it does not follow that I blindly support every act committed by those calling themselves Muslims, whether they are acts committed individually or collectively. To this end, I firmly believe that I am supported by my faith, which exhorts me to forbid evil and enjoin good, no matter which "side" it may be coming from.

Unfortunately, some Muslims have fallen into the trap of too easily overlooking crimes committed by their own, and focusing on those committed by others. A regrettable side effect of this is the victim mentality with which so many Muslims are afflicted, and, which, over time, reduces the efficacity and dynamism of a community. To me, this is against the very essence of Islam, which makes it very clear that the responsibility that comes with our free will is very much part of the bargain. By blaming others for our misfortunes, we are shirking that responsibility, and ignoring the Quran:

> God has promised to those among you who believe, and work righteous deeds, that He will of a surety grant them in the land, inheritance (of power), as He granted it to those before them; that He will establish in authority their religion (deen), the one which He has chosen for them; and that He will change (their state), after the fear in which they (lived), to one of security and peace. (24:55)

This appears to be a promise in the clearest terms. Worldly power, security, peace and the prevailing of their way of life, is promised to those who "believe, and work righteous deeds". Muslims need to ask themselves who possesses these benefits in the world, and why. There is no room in the above verse for blaming others. Rather, it is the plainest of exhortations that if you do the work then you will get the reward. That, of course, does not absolve others from blame when they wrong you. But your responsibility lies with those matters within your control.

So, as the above verse states, how we live our lives is crucial to our success not only in the Hereafter, but also here on earth. And how we live our lives will be influenced in no small part by our value system. Whether we admit it or not, we all live by certain values. Even if we choose to deny that there is any ethical or moral imperative in life, that itself is an assertion of the values by which we have chosen to live. In each generation, no doubt issues will arise which lead us to assert or question our values. The evil that had to be confronted in the form of Hitler, for example, was an assertion of our value system in the last century. More recently, the way we have reacted to the MPs' expenses scandals, and the greed of bankers, shows that there is still something within the human psyche that objects to immoral conduct.

It may just be that such objections are harder to bring to the surface in societies which place over themselves as many insulating layers as we seem to do now. Materialism, in its various forms, muffles the sound of those objections. The Western world has enjoyed unprecedented prosperity in recent times, which has served to dull our senses and increase our apathy. It is not an exaggeration to suggest that in modern Western societies we are encouraged to become addicted, and consequently distracted. Whether it be illicit drugs or legal ones, football or reality television, we are bombarded with inane activity which further removes us from those things that should matter. As long as we get our regular fix of these opiates, we can see out our lives in relative contentment. Perhaps those who compare these distractions with the gladiatorial contests of Imperial Rome have a point, given the decline that seems to be facing the West now.

The question arises, therefore, where our values should come from. Ironically, the proposed answer here – religion – has, itself, been regarded as an opiate. This accusation, regrettably, is not without foundation. It cannot be denied that there are those who have used it to control the masses; history has many examples of people imposing religion on others for political ends. And, often, even those who have chosen to adopt religion of their own free will have all too readily conceded their autonomy as human beings. They may well have held genuine and sincere beliefs, but they have too frequently allowed others, supposedly more religiously qualified or knowledgeable, to speak for them, and – perhaps more worryingly – think for them, too. In recent times, we have seen at close quarters the direction in which this can lead a minority of extremist followers. They can be the cause of much damage to society, but that is nothing compared to the damage they inflict on the religion they purport to follow. This valid criticism of religion as an opiate, however, should not mask the fact that other ways of life can also be used to control the masses. How often, for example, have we seen crimes being committed in the name of democracy? The very invocation of that word stifles any criticism from the outset.

The danger is not religion itself, any more than it is any other way of life. Rather, is in the abdication of personal responsibility in both thought and deed. Islam, contrary to the views of many of its critics, does not advocate such an abdication of personal responsibility. It is, of course, central to this faith that humans are ultimately account-able before their Creator, but this does not mean that every sphere of human life is, or should be, governed by so-called "religious" rules. Many Muslims, themselves, are blissfully unaware that for many centuries Muslim scholars were not afraid to question even the most fundamental beliefs and practices of and by Islam. Nowadays, even the slightest deviation from orthodoxy is met with accusations of blasphemy and infidelity.

It is no coincidence, however, that that era of Muslim debate and dissension coincided with an era of military and material strength, and the psychological security that it brought with it. Now, when many Muslims feel under attack, and, therefore, assume a siege mentality, they become unnecessarily defensive, and retreat to the perceived safety of orthodoxy. Everything becomes either black or white, because – with all the uncertainty around them, the grappling with new cultures and languages, the military superiority of other nations, the educational shortcomings of many Muslim nations, and the incessant negative media coverage of all things Islamic – the one area they regard as a safe haven is their faith. Others may well criticise it, or even ridicule it, but for Muslims, it provides something firmly rooted and reassuring in a world that is changing at an ever-increasing rate. Muslims have to wake up, however, and understand exactly what it is that they have turned Islam into – and what it should be. Is it just a system of comforting rituals, which really does act as an opiate, taking away the pain of the real world? Or, is it, in fact, a way of life that urges constant endeavour and action to improve ourselves individually and collectively, to tackle problems rather than shy away from them, all the while remembering that, ultimately, we are answerable to the Almighty? Does it recognise that there is more to life than the physical and material components we can empirically assess; is it an holistic way of life that does not compartmentalise the physical and the spiritual, but accepts that both should play a role in the creation of the successful individual, and thereby, society? If this is what Islam is, or should be, can it be so without any active involvement on the part of its followers? Is it a readymade mix, requiring no further input from believers, which can simply be applied, like an ointment, to our wounds? Or is there a role, and a significant one at that, for Muslims themselves?

There is nothing wrong with the Muslim belief that the Islamic way of life should emanate from the guidance provided to humanity by God Himself. The Quran is where we should look for this guidance, bearing in mind that we are more than just passive recipients of this revelation. It is not by accident that we have been endowed with the most complex and powerful of faculties in the shape of our brain, the full capabilities of which we still do not understand. It does not make sense that we would be given this powerful tool if all that we were expected to do was passively receive the guidance and implement it without any thought of our own. Furthermore, is it perhaps rational to think that maybe one reason we have been given such capable brains is that the problems facing us do not remain the same, but constantly change, and, therefore, require new and innovative solutions? We have the intellectual capacity to come up with those solutions but, being human, when left to our own devices we also have the ability to come up with creations which are more harmful than beneficial to society and, therefore, we are very much in need of guidance. It is entirely reasonable to conclude that such guidance comes best from an objective, external source, one that is familiar with our workings and knows what is best for us, despite ourselves.

The Quran provides that guidance, and, although it could have been, it is not *The Million Commandments*. It is believed by Muslims to be the direct word of God, revealed over the course of 23 years to the Prophet Muhammad, through the angel Gabriel. Now, if God had so desired, he could have simply dictated commandment after commandment (and there was time for plenty over the course of almost a quarter of a century). Yet, He did not. The Quran is not the ultimate rulebook. It contains many similes and parables. Much of it is allegorical. It covers specific, contemporaneous instances as well as general examples from history. Many of its themes are repeated. This, to the outsider – especially one not familiar with the language or cultural idiom involved – can lead to the erroneous conclusion that it is a bit of a muddle which has extensively borrowed from other religions. Such conclusions are amateurish, and do not take account of the basic requirement of the Quran: namely, that it requires its reader to think. Time and again it instructs us to ponder our surroundings. Not only does this help us to understand its similes, its historical and scientific examples, and, thereby, its Divine authorship, but it should also lead us to reflect on why it is that the Quran is not simply a rulebook.

We need to be able to distinguish between the values of our faith and individual laws that apply to a particular time and place. If the requirements of society so dictate, the latter can be modified, as long as the underlying value system is adhered to. There are those Muslims, for example, who insist that music is forbidden in Islam. I do not believe that it is; there is certainly no verse to that effect in the Quran. More importantly, however, we need to ask what Islamic value it offends; when we do, the discussion becomes more nuanced. Militant rap music advocating violence and the sexual objectification of women clearly offends against several Islamic values, so one can appreciate any argument suggesting it ought to be shunned. But it is difficult for me to accept that all forms of music, even the most exquisite of classical pieces, are forbidden according to my faith. As it happens, I love listening to music. It can be inspirational and uplifting, or simply relaxing and enjoyable. It clearly brings joy to my children, who share my eclectic musical taste, which includes everything from Guns n' Roses to Sami Yusuf, The Elgins to The Prodigy. (There was a time when my son would wander round the house singing along happily to Frank Sinatra's "Love and Marriage", but he would always sing "hope and marriage" instead, and I had to constantly remind him that there was no hope!) How could I accept an interpretation of Islam that excluded such a beautiful part of life? There is a tradition that Prophet said, "God is beautiful, and loves beauty." We need to think long and hard before legislating prohibitively.

We also need to remember that even such laws as there are in Islam are not ends in themselves. They are meant to assist us on our path towards God, our ultimate destination or return, and their observance is of little use if it does not help us along that path. Islam is not supposed to be a religion for box-tickers. It is supposed to be the blueprint for the "civilising mission" which is what humanity is all about. Religion should inspire us to seek always the improvement of the human race, yet, so often our behaviour suggests we are going backwards. It is sometimes regarded as a sign of liberal enlightenment and progress when music and films contain more expletives than they used to, when women wear less and less in the name of choice, and when life is generally characterised by fewer inhibitions. Yet this trend leads us back to where we started: naked and coarse, like the cavemen we once were. Progress indeed. We need to consider which direction we should be moving in, individually and collectively, and consider which social constructs assist us in that regard, and which hinder us.

We Muslims have created a multitude of rules for ourselves. We have "rules" for every aspect of life, including sitting down, standing up, walking, talking – in short, every type of action and interaction that it is humanly possible to achieve. There are different categories of edict – from the mandatory, through the desirable, to the voluntary – yet next to none of these emanate from the Quran itself. There are, of course, secondary sources in which certain of these "rules" can be found. But the basic commandment is quite simply this: heed the Quran. When we do so, we find a book which is of practical value not because it contains rules for every last detail of life, but because of the general guidance it offers. Indeed, the general principles themselves are often not readily apparent, but are arrived at as the result of a process of reflection. Further, one has to have an understanding of the historical context in order to appreciate fully what is meant by certain verses appearing to contain specific commands. Anybody seeking to understand the Quran properly has to understand that it will take some effort, but also that we have been endowed with the capacity to make such effort. Life should be about constant positive human effort, and, in this regard, it is inevitable that such positive effort will reap its rewards in our understanding of the Quran.

It is from this process of applying ourselves to a contextual analysis of the Quran that we can hope to derive the general principles to apply to our modern lives. We can ascertain what have been described as the "Divine objectives", and see how they were implemented at the time of the revelation, but then we need to consider the needs of our own societies. It is certainly not intrinsic to Islam that all the rules which were applied in 7th-century Arabia are relevant to 21st-century Britain, or America, or even any modern Muslim state. Those who think that the "Shariah" is a system of laws which is set in stone have misunderstood the meaning of the word. In order to legislate effectively and in accordance with Islam, we have to understand the needs we are legislating for and this requires us to develop an anthropological understanding of our society. One cannot legislate in the field of genetic engineering, for example, by having knowledge of the scriptures, and none about the science at issue. In adopting this considered approach, we can begin to take the first tentative steps away from thinking of Islam as a relic of the past, concerned solely with ritual worship, and towards making it relevant to our society.

There is an important Quranic lesson that illuminates this point. The prohibition on alcohol is a famous Islamic "rule", yet the way in which it came to be prohibited is highly instructive. There are three significant verses relating to alcohol in the Quran. The first states that alcohol (like gambling) causes some good and some harm, but that the harm outweighs the good. The second relevant verse exhorts people not to come to the mosques intoxicated, which was clearly something the Arabs at the time were not averse to doing. The third verse states that alcohol should be avoided altogether. Now, it was well within the power of the Almighty simply to announce in the first revelation that alcohol was forbidden, but He did not, and it is incumbent upon us to question why. The only sensible explanation is that the society in question was simply not ready for that prohibition, so, rather than issue a commandment that would be ignored, the Almighty, in His infinite wisdom, prepared the society for the eventual demise of this habit. "Prohibition" is exactly the right word, as it brings to mind the period of American history during which alcohol was unsuccessfully prohibited: that society was neither ready nor willing to desist from its consumption. Contrast that to the recent banning of cigarette smoking in many public places in the West; not a blanket prohibition, but the first steps on a course which will ultimately persuade and prepare society to accept, for itself, that cigarette smoking is to be avoided. If at some stage in the future a law is passed "prohibiting" it, society will have evolved enough for it to more readily accept such a law.

This approach to Islam is advocated by many so-called reformists – and here is another area fraught with difficulty. "Reform" has become a dirty word for many Muslims. I recall a few years ago attending a lecture by Tariq Ramadan on the topic of Reformation in Islam. Outside the building, I was met by some very smart young Muslims who were handing out various leaflets. I assumed they were part of his young, educated following and that they were handing me some information about the lecture. I was somewhat shocked to discover, therefore, that the leaflets were essentially saying that Islam does not need any reformation. What, exactly, do we mean by reform? The above suggested approach to the Quran, and the way we should legislate for our society, is arguably little more than common sense. Yet the fact that it may attract the ire of many Muslims highlights the stagnation of our thinking. Any type of change is condemned without thinking about exactly what it is that is being found objectionable. Scholars such as Ramadan who are straining every synapse to work out how Islam can remain relevant to our society, are condemned by those who regard thinking as optional. Such people demonstrate a conservatism which may help them cope with the demands of modern society, but they fail to realise what they leave behind. Their own children end up either just going through the motions of religion, or adopting ultra-conservative and insular positions which do them no service in today's world, or simply abandoning their faith. Non-Muslims look at Islam from the outside and see nothing useful to their lives; they think it is a faith which, if anything, discourages free thinking. Ultimately, the very idea of reform in Islam is left to a select group of academics, and the rest of the community carries on regardless.

This has to change. It may be that people view the word "reform" itself as objectionable. Fine. Find another word. The word does not matter. What is of crucial importance is the approach it purports to advocate, namely, thinking about one's faith. It does not mean looking at one's faith through the eyes of Arabs in the 7th century, but through contemporary eyes, assisted with the latest knowledge about their environment. Muslims need to have at the forefront of their minds the constant Quranic reminders to reflect, and use their powers of reason, and if they can do so sincerely and determinedly, then there is hope for the future of Islam. And this approach is not the sole preserve of academics. The Ed Husains of the world, and their Quilliam organisations, which have damaged their credibility with so many Muslims, need to be shown that the followers of the faith can think for themselves, and do not need "sell-out" organisations to lead the way. Those like Irshad Manji should be shown that Muslims are not the stereotypical, backwards caricatures that she invokes, and do not need to be insulted and have the very foundations of their faith undermined in order for them to keep that faith relevant today. And those neo-con cheerleaders like Ayaan Hersi Ali will naturally fall by the wayside if a new movement for thinking in Islam captures the collective Muslim imagination.

None of this is possible without the firm foundations provided by an education – for men *and* women. How much longer can Muslims, in some parts of the world, justify wilfully ignoring half of their community's talents, abilities and ideas? If a woman is a man's equal in the eyes of God, which she certainly is according to the Quran, is it not reasonable to expect that she be his equal when viewed through his own eyes? The answer is obvious, even if in some quarters it is long overdue. Too many Muslims, particularly men, have failed to take advantage of the educational facilities available to them, especially in the West, and for this failure they will one day have to account. Not only have they squandered opportunities for themselves and their families, but they have also done a great disservice to their faith. They struggle to distinguish their religion from their inherited cultural baggage. And if they are not clear themselves, how can they criticise others who, mistakenly but understandably, confuse honour killings, forced marriages, female genital mutilation, and other culturally driven social deficiencies, with Islam, i.e. submission to the Creator? The sad fact is that too few of us have an understanding of Islam beyond following a few of its rules.

Another negative result of many Muslims' lack of education is their susceptibility to being "played", or their gullibility. It has almost become a sick joke that if you want to get Muslims to start rioting and end up killing each other, all you have to do is press their buttons. Say something offensive about their Prophet and leave the rest to them. That Prophet, who patiently bore insult after insult, would probably be turning in His grave at the thought of what certain Muslims are doing in the name of safeguarding His "dignity". There is little doubt that the absence of useful knowledge and critical understanding plays a part in the mindless riots orchestrated in certain parts of the world whenever such "offences" come to light. The organisers often have their own motives for these demonstrations of religious objection, but the fact that their populations have little in the way of education leaves them open to manipulation.

Such manipulation comes in many guises. There are those who are ill-disposed towards Islam and Muslims, and exploit sensitivities about matters deemed to be sacred. And then there are certain leaders in Muslim countries who manipulate their populations' indignation at, for example, perceived offences from non-Muslims. The conclusion that even the most enlightened of Muslims now reach, however, is that the media plays the most significant part in exacerbating the problem, knowing full well that there is a ready ear for negative stories about Muslims. A vicious cycle develops in which negative media reporting creates anti-Muslim sentiment, which is then fed by further negative media reporting. The result is an atmosphere so pernicious that rational thinking is jettisoned, and heels are dug into respective positions. The collective mood of the nation has by now become so moulded by these opinion makers that, when the usual stereotypes are highlighted, people look no further than the obvious explanations. Media sound bites prevail over proper analysis, with the result that nothing is learned from the last century, and we are more than content to sit back and watch one particular community become the scapegoat.

The seeds of the later (and justifiable) complaints of rational Muslims were, in part, sown in the Seventies and Eighties, with the subconscious racism and anti-Muslim sentiment created by seemingly innocuous action B-movies from Hollywood (such as the prodigious output of messrs Menahem Golan and Yoram Globus), which invariably portrayed Muslims, or Arabs, as either terrorists or useless playboy millionaires. That kind of culture helps to form a nation's psyche in such a way that subsequently, when it becomes expedient to point the finger at a particular group, society is ready to accept unquestioningly that group's guilt. The recent example of the men convicted of grooming young girls for sexual exploitation in England is highly instructive.

Certain sections of the media emphasised the religion of the offenders, as if it played a part in their offending, and as if they were typical examples of their faith communities. And, as this particular dog had already been given a bad name, its ill-treatment was going to raise little in the way of objection. It was another tawdry episode relating to Muslims, who, as we have seen, have no redeeming features, individually or collectively. The fears and insecurities of non-Muslims are exploited, fuelled by the amplification of the misdeeds of certain Muslims. Any hope of inter-community harmony is extinguished as people are separated into rival camps. This "divide and rule" tactic works on so many levels, leaving the powers that be safe to keep ruling while the masses are preoccupied with fighting each other.

A particularly illuminating example of how society can be moulded in such a way that it asks no questions when the "usual suspects" are blamed, is that of "Revolution Muslim" in the United States. It is a story you would struggle to make up, but, as ever, truth proves stranger than fiction. The creators of *South Park*, the American cartoon series, decided to depict the Prophet Muhammad in the 200th episode of their show. It was not particularly offensive, but that did not stop a radical group known as "Revolution Muslim", based in New York, issuing threats against the *South Park* creators, suggesting that their actions would result in their untimely deaths. No surprises there, you may think, given how mad Muslims obviously are. Unsurprisingly, CNN picked up the story, and decided to give it much publicity, thereby implying that this group was somehow representative of Muslims. So far, so predictable. But this is where things began to get interesting.

The founder of the radical group was one Yousef al-Khattab, whose real name was Joseph Cohen. Cohen was born and raised in the United States as a Jew, and held both American and Israeli citizenship. In the late Eighties, Cohen embraced an ultra-orthodox interpretation of Judaism, and began attending a *yeshiva* (rabbinical school). In 1998, Cohen, like many American Zionist Jews before him, packed his bags and relocated to the Israeli Occupied Territories, where he became a settler. An ardent Zionist, Cohen fell in with the Jewish fundamentalist group *Shas*, an extreme right-wing political party. Yet, less than three years later, he had "converted" to Islam, having had some online chat with a radical Muslim cleric who, having clearly worked his magic on this particular Zionist, you might think would have used his powers of persuasion on the rest of Israel and promptly solved the Middle East conflict with just his trusty webcam. But alas not.

Cohen/al-Khattab moved back to the United States, and founded the most radical Islamic group in the country. This is, as far as I am aware, the first time such a committed Zionist has switched to radical Islam. Together with his side-kick Younis Muhammad – a similarly mysterious "convert" to Islam from extreme Zionism – they formed "Revolution Muslim" and, despite their conversion to a new faith, began to adopt an agenda which could only have been authored by somebody with a real hatred of Islam. For example, one of them claimed that the Quran commands terrorism: just the type of comment that a hard-core Islamophobe would want to announce to the world. Considering the founder's background in an extreme right-wing fundamentalist Israeli political party, Muslims have every reason to be suspicious.

"Revolution Muslim" was just too convenient, but that did not stop the media portraying those two "Muslims" as representative of millions of Muslim Americans. Cohen/al-Khattab was giving the mainstream media the narrative they wanted to hear, namely that Muslims are violent and irrational, and simply lose their minds when the Prophet Muhammad is depicted. And this was a message that society had been well prepared to receive.

"Revolution Muslim" is an extreme example, but there are plenty of instances of more subtle games being played with an all-too-gullible Muslim community. For the last few years, Sufism has been a much-discussed topic in the Western world, and the circumstances of the discussion are cause for some concern. To many Muslims, Sufism represents the mystical or spiritual essence of their faith – what they would regard as the reality, the substance of faith, rather than the mere form of outward obedience. It is regarded as properly understood and practised by those who are devout and sincere, and have more than a passing acquaintance with Islam. To some, however, it is seen as a rejection of all worldly matters and a retreat into a more spiritual place. This is essentially a debate that exists in other faiths, too – the tension between form and substance, the material and spiritual – and one can appreciate that it is a debate which is properly addressed by only the more deep thinking of individuals. Yet during the anti-extremism drive in post-7/7 Britain, it became quite a popular topic of discussion.

Now, it may have been that it was an entirely sincere discussion, and I am just another unduly suspicious and paranoid Muslim. But I was somewhat surprised at the increasing frequency of people asking me whether or not I was from the Sufi branch of Islam. My answer usually began with a slightly surprised explanation of how I did not particularly describe myself as Sufi, nor indeed feel the need for such labels. I would then go on to explain that although I did appreciate, and agree, with the Sufi emphasis on valuing the reality rather than the outward manifestation, in my view that did not mean that Islam advocated shunning this world. Monasticism played no part in Islam, which as far as I was concerned encourages man to get involved in society, albeit with the caveat that the ultimate reality lies elsewhere and this world is merely a test. Then I would go away thinking how bizarre it was that Sufism seemed to crop up so regularly in conversation and that, often, when I was asked about it, I got the impression that the questioner rather hoped I would say I was a Sufi. My fear was that there was a drive in certain quarters to promote Sufism, not out of any concern for the spiritual essence of Islam, but as an underhand attempt to depoliticise Muslims by persuading them that their faith was really an apolitical one which, if anything, advocated the conscious avoidance of involvement in worldly affairs. This message would struggle to gain acceptance if it was imposed, or even suggested, from outside the community, so tactically it would need to be promoted from within.

This suspicion was heightened when I became aware of the controversy surrounding Haris Rafiq and the Sufi Muslim Council. Once again, the truth is perhaps a little blurry, but what we can say for sure is that a new Muslim organisation appeared, that it had the backing of the government of the day (hardly a ringing endorsement given that government's other follies) and was supposed to be a counter to the Muslim Council of Britain. So, for an organisation claiming to represent the "apolitical" side of Islam, it had got off to a particularly political start. It even had the former British ambassador to Uzbekistan, Craig Murray, accusing it of being linked to American neo-conservative organisations, which hardly seemed consistent with the peace-loving Sufism it claimed to represent. In fact, as many people pointed out, genuine Sufis do not describe themselves as such anyway, preferring to concentrate privately on purifying their inner selves rather than establishing organisations in a public space. Whatever the truth behind this organisation, what we can safely say is that, in the six or seven years it has been going, despite its suggestion that 80 per cent of British Muslims are from a Sufi background, it has hardly managed to rally them under its apolitical banner, and has fallen by the wayside, like many other unrepresentative groupings before it. Government support and funding are wonderful things, but perhaps the lesson is that they only take you so far.

Such examples are simply the ones that are exposed; it hardly needs to be said that it is in the nature of such schemes that their origins should remain undisclosed. Muslims (and, in fact, the rest of society) need to be alert to the sinister games that are being played out there. To be fair, it is not only the Muslims who are the victims of such games, but for some time now, they seem to have been on the receiving end more often than others.

However, although a degree of scepticism is undoubtedly in order, Muslims need to move beyond pointing the finger at others, and begin to recognise and act upon their own failings. They must avoid being gullible, and reacting so predictably so often. They need to develop a greater confidence when dealing with others, which does not come from shouting the loudest – something that, regrettably, we are highly proficient at – but from knowing one's position in the world, one's values and one's purpose. The assertion of Muslim values thereafter should not be the hollow, often hypocritical mantra "it's against our religion", which we hear all too regularly, but, in fact, should be in actions rather than words. I imagine if we Muslims truly lived according to the values we espouse, there would be very little that we would have to say, and the "Revolution Muslims" of this world would not find such receptive ears so easily.

Muslims also need to realise that they are not alone in holding certain values. There are billions of people in the world who believe in a Supreme Being, who believe that they will be held accountable for their actions in this world, and who believe that there is such a thing as morality, and that it is a force for good which needs to govern our actions. Muslims can claim no exclusivity over this. If God is the sea, and the differing religions are the rivers leading to that sea, then it may be that Muslims can claim that their river is the one which provides the most straightforward access to the sea, with the fewest obstacles. This does not render the other faiths untrue or meaningless; in fact, the Quran says as much. And even if we have been blessed with the clearest tributary leading to God, this in itself has not prevented some of us doing our best to introduce obstacles into it and, pardon the pun, to muddy the waters. These are the perennial human failings which have constantly added to, diluted, explained and otherwise addressed the simple

Divine commandments, and thereby introduced the man-made into religion. This does not mean that religion itself has no basis, just that that basis is often ignored, or departed from, and needs to be returned to and rethought in every generation.

Once we establish that we hold certain values in common, we need to make a concerted effort to formalise that understanding by building alliances with others. It is difficult enough to live according to religious values in modern society, but doing so alone is much more difficult than doing so with the support of the community around you. This applies not just to individuals, but also to groups. Much more would be achieved if Muslims were able to call on their counterparts in other faiths, particularly Judaism and Christianity, and show a united front. This has to start with conversation, and with the building of friendships as foundations. How appalling is it that relations with Jews, who at one stage in history used to seek sanctuary in Muslim countries, are at such a low ebb that many people believe enmity has always been the defining feature of the Jewish-Muslim relationship. Efforts towards friendship need to be initiated, appreciated and reciprocated.

One of my proudest moments was when I was asked to be a godfather/spiritual friend after my close friends, Steven and Anya, had their baby daughter Jemima. Their Christianity did not prevent them seeing qualities in me which they felt justified the offer of such a role, and then approaching their vicar to see how they could make it happen. Happily, my Islam recognised and appreciated the friendship and love that was being offered, and was thrilled to accept the invitation. And although relationships like this may start on a personal level, the possibilities thereafter are endless. There is no reason why they cannot help create strong, compassionate, unified, yet diverse communities. The sadness often arises not between individuals, but when those with the power and influence to bring communities together neglect to do so. I still find it shameful that the British Council, for example, can create a booklet called *Our Shared Europe*, to assist with social cohesion efforts on the continent by recalling the historical contributions of Muslims in Europe, yet fail to see how this publication could be a powerful tool for bringing British youngsters together in our own schools.

There are so many issues on which a common approach is warranted. Regrettably, there is often a lazy assumption on the part of some Muslims that what is not obviously "Muslim" must somehow be inferior. This most often applies to social behaviour; as far as many Muslims are concerned, Western culture is defined by prejudice, drunkenness and debauchery. Not only is this hypocritical – overlooking the blatant racism and caste and tribal discrimination in many Muslim societies, as well as levels of immorality that would make the average "infidel" blush – but it is also erroneous. It was not without good cause that an Islamic scholar once remarked, upon returning to his country from the West, that "there I saw Islam but no Muslims, here I see Muslims but no Islam". He had rightly observed the implementation in Western countries of "Islamic" values such as fairness, tolerance, honesty, a lack of corruption, and welfare provision for the needy, with not a Muslim in sight. Yet, when he returned to a land rich with Muslims, he found it poor in all the values that Muslims should stand for. We need to move beyond an understanding of morality which restricts itself to personal (usually sexual) behaviour while ignoring the incessant corruption evident in much of our governance.

Muslims can also learn from others who have already had to grapple with reconciling religious belief with the demands of modern life, and can now share their experiences and knowledge. Just as a thousand years ago many non-Muslims benefited from knowledge which was in the hands of Muslims, so, too, Muslims now need to realise that they can similarly benefit from the knowledge and experience of others, without this meaning a dilution of their own beliefs. They can find those who share their values, and tackle together the many difficulties faced by society today. When the bankers ran off with taxpayers' money, they could not have cared less if the bailout came from a Muslim, Christian or atheist source. Similarly, when "austerity" measures are imposed by governments seeking to placate the world of finance, they do not discriminate between believer and non-believer. These, and other pressing social issues, need to be tackled by those with the expertise to do so. The wider this grouping, the more chance it has of success.

Insofar as Muslims become involved in such tasks, as they should, they need to do so without resorting to a dogmatic approach to faith, which no longer works, and in any event was never supposed to be the Islamic way. In addressing these and other concerns, they can hope to recreate the success story of Cordoba a thousand years ago. They can attempt to create a society with mutual cooperation for mutual benefit; a society that does not have such a gulf between the haves and have-nots; a society where tolerance means more than simply putting up with each other;

in short, a society which should be the norm, but sadly is becoming a more distant prospect with the passing of each day.

❧ ❧ ❧

The day after the 7/7 bombings in London, I was asked to do *Pause for Thought* on BBC Radio 2. I was as appalled and upset as the next person about what had happened, and certainly did not think that I had any great insights to offer. But, after some hesitation, I agreed. I spoke of being united in grief with the rest of the nation, my nation. I made it clear that I followed Islam and prayed five times a day. But that I also checked the Liverpool FC website five times a day, too. And that what defined me was my humanity.

At the time I was the chair of the Merseyside Council of Faiths, which received a letter from an English lady who had listened to that particular *Pause for Thought*, and felt compelled to write, to commend me on what I had said, and to say it had made her feel "proud" that I was British. I found her comments uplifting. But the fact remained: I had done nothing special. I was, after all, just your average Muslim.

Suggested Further Reading

Akbar, Ahmed, Jinnah, *Pakistan and Islamic Identity*

Al-Ghazali, Abu Hamid, *The Alchemy of Happiness*

Armstrong, Karen, *Islam, A Short History*

Armstrong, Karen, *Muhammad*

Aslan, Reza, *No God but God*

Blum, William, *Rogue State*

Bryson, Bill, *A Short History of Nearly Everything*

Chomsky, Noah, *Deterring Democracy*

Chomsky, Noah, *The Fateful Triangle*

David, Ron, *Arabs and Israel for Beginners*

El-Affendi, Abdelwahab, *Who Needs an Islamic State?*

El Diwany, Tarek, *The Problem with Interest*

El Fadl, Khaled Abou, *The Great Theft*

Esack, Farid, *On Being Muslim*

Freely, John, *Light from the East*

Graham, Mark, *How Islam Created the Modern World*

Hobson, John, *The Eastern Origins of Western Civilisation*

Iqbal, Muhammad, *The Reconstruction of Religious Thought in Islam*

Klein, Naomi, *The Shock Doctrine*

Kushner, Tony, *and Solomon, Alisa, Wrestling with Zion*
Lings, Martin, *Muhammad*
Lyons, Jonathan, *The House of Wisdom*
Menocal, Maria, *The Ornament of the World*
Morgan, Michael, *Lost History*
Nasr, Seyyed Hossein, *The Heart of Islam*
Palast, Greg, *The Best Democracy Money Can Buy*
Perkins, John, *Confessions of an Economic Hitman*
Saeed, Abdullah, *Interpreting the Quran*
Safi, Omid, *Progressive Muslims*
Sardar, Zia, *Desperately Seeking Paradise*
Thomas, Abdulkader, *Interest in Islamic Economics*
Vidal, Gore, *Perpetual War for Perpetual Peace*
Wadud, Amina, *Inside the Gender Jihad*
Wadud, Amina, *Quran and Woman*

Index

7/7 London bombings 212
9/11 New York attacks 13, 179–80

Abdullah Quilliam Society 180–81
Afghanistan 35, 59, 123, 128–9
agnosticism 76
Al-Battani, Muhammad ibn Jabir al-Harrani 90, 105
alcohol 48, 105, 197–8, 210
algebra 88, 105
Algeria 111
Al-Haytham, Abu Ali al-Hasan Ibn (Alhazen) 96–7, 105
Ali, Ayaan Hirsi 172–3, 200
Al-Kindi, Yaqub Ibn Ishaq 88, 94
Allende, Salvador 137–8
Al-Razi, Muhammad ibn Zakaria 94–5
Alton, David, MP 45
America, United States of 112–13, 116, 151
  interventions in Muslim coun tries 116–19, 123
  positive view of 186–9
  pro-capitalist agenda 136–42
  support for Israel 124–7
  undermining of democracies 137–41
anaesthetic 95
Arab Spring demonstrations 114, 133
Arabic 62–3; see also numerals
Arbenz, Jacobo 138–9
Armstrong, Karen 175
Arnold-Craft, Peter 43
arts 66, 77

Aslan, Reza 177, 182
astronomy 89–92
atheism 65, 136
Azerbaijan 93

Baghdad 86, 95, 103
Balochistan 122–3
Bangladesh 130
banks/banking 146, 150–53, 158-9, 190
Bayt al Hikmah (House of Wisdom) 86, 88, 177
BBC Radio 212
Begin, Menachem 126
Berlin Wall 135
Beverly Hills Cop 186
Bhutto, Zukfikar Ali 35
The Bible, the Quran and Science 62
Bin Laden, Osama 121–2
biology 70–72
Birmingham, described as a Muslim city 9–10
Blue Coat School, Liverpool 41–4
BNP (British Nationalist Party) 29
Body of Lies 188
Boeing 152
Bosch, Juan 140
brain 68, 70
Brazil 140
Brierfield, Lancashire 21, 33
British Council 210
Bryson, Bill 74
Bucaille, Maurice 62, 77–8
Buddhism 157
Bush, George W. 108

Cairo 86, 95, 103
capitalism 136, 141, 142, 146
cars 19–20, 25–6, 40
cartoons depicting Prophet
  Muhammad 163–4
caste system 27–9, 210
Charlie Hebdo killings 9
Chaudhry, Mohammad Din (Zia's
  father) 21-6, 31-3, 39-40, 57-8
Chaudhry, Zia
  early childhood in East
    Lancashire 25–32
  later childhood in Liverpool
    32-48
  student at Manchester University
    47, 48–53
  law career 44-5, 53–6
Chavez, Hugo 141
chemical weapons 114–15
chemistry 94
children, behaviour standards 44,
  49, 59–60
Chile, American-backed coup
  137–8
China 80–81, 120, 123, 157
CHiPs 185
Chomsky, Noam 126
Christianity 29, 52, 84, 108
  Coptic 110, 130
Churchill, Winston 114–15
CIA 120–21, 137, 139–40
Circle of Literary Friends 45
CNN 203
Cohen, Joseph (Yousef al-Khattab)
  204–5
Cold War 118, 136
colonialism 111, 115-16
Communism 118–19, 135-7, 141
consciousness 75

Constantinople, fall of 84
consumerism 15, 142
Copernicus, Nicolaus 93, 97, 105
Cordoba 83, 86, 95–6, 99, 103,
  104, 130, 177, 211
corruption 48, 211
'Creation myth' 66–7
Crusades 108–11, 129–30
Cuba 139, 140–41

Daesh *see* ISIS (Islamic State)
Dallas 185
Damascus 86, 95, 103
Dante Alighieri 84
Dark Ages 83–4
Datsun 20, 40
Dawkins, Richard 65
debt 143, 146–50
democracy 65, 117, 120, 124, 126,
  132, 137–41, 153, 190
Desperately Seeking Paradise 35
DNA 72–4
Dominican Republic 140
drugs 190
Dukes of Hazzard 185
Dynasty 185

East Lancashire *see* Lancashire
East Timor 128
economy 15, 142–3, 147-8, 151
Ecuador 140
Eden, Anthony 118
Egypt 112, 118, 120–21
Eid 82
El Diwany, Tarek 146, 149
El Fadl, Khalid Abou 182
El Salvador 139–40
embryology 78
entrepreneurialism 26

environment 142, 148, 156
evidence 67-8, 74
evolution 52
expletives 196

faith 15–6, 67–8
Fallujah 115
fasting 168–9
Fatimids of Egypt 109
films 188, 196, 202
financial crisis 150–51
fingerprints 74
Fitzgerald, Edward 91
food 27
football 54, 190, 212
Ford Cortina 19–20
free speech 51
freedom 65, 120

Gaddafi, Colonel Muammar 114
Galileo Galilei 97
gas 123
Gaza 126
Geber (Jabir ibn Hayyan) 93–4
genetics 73–4
genital mutilation 201
Gerard of Cremona 96, 98
Glaspie, April 112
globalisation 151–2
God
    as Creator 70–75
    rationality of believing in 61–79
gold 123
Goldline Taxis 27
Goldsmith, Lord 39
Goulart, Joao 140
Greeks, ancient 85
Gregorian calendar 91
Guatemala 138–9

Gujjar caste 27–9, 33–4
Gwadar 123

haemophilia 96
Halliburton 113
Harris, David, QC 54
Harvey, William 101–2, 105
hijab 30, 37
Hinduism 28
history 82–4, 129, 177
    Islamic Golden Age 84–106,
    177
Hitchens, Christopher 65
Hitler, Adolf 190
honour 28, 201
Hubble telescope 91
human rights, as an Islamic
    concept 132
Humanism 84
Hurd, Douglas, MP 51
Husain, Ed 60, 172, 178–81, 200
Hussein, Saddam 112, 115, 141

Ibn Nafis, Ala al-Din 100–102
Ibn Rushd, Abu'l Walid (Averroes)
    99–100, 104
Ibn Sina, Abu Ali al-Ḥusayn ibn
    Abd Allah (Avicenna) 97–8, 100
Ibn Zuhr, Abu Marwan Abd-al-
    Malik (Avenzoar) 98-100
imams 31, 50–51
immorality 210–11
immunology 95
imperialism 115–18, 123, 126
independence movements 115, 116
India 48, 80, 85, 111, 127-9, 141
Indonesia 118
inheritance 87
interest (banking) 147–9

inter-faith connections 14, 58, 81–2, 208–9
International Monetary Fund 149
Iqbal, Mohammed 23, 46, 48
Iran 59, 86, 117-21, 124-5
Iran, Shah of (Mohammad Reza Pahlavi) 120, 141
Iran-Iraq War 130
Iraq 108, 111-13, 120, 131
ISIS (Islamic State) 10
Islam
    criticisms of 'reform' 16–7, 196–200
    critics of 141, 172–4
    different ways of practising 59
    Golden Age 84–106, 177
    relevance to modern life 165–72
    spread of 84–5
    wider social role 13, 15–16
Islamic Banking 158–9
The Islamist 59, 179–80
Islamophobia 182
Israel 124–7, 132-3, 178
Italy 84

Jerusalem 108–9
Jewish community 82, 109, 127
jihad 35
Jinnah, Mohammed Ali 22–3, 46, 48, 128
Judaism 157, 204

Kashmir 128
Kassem, Abdul Karim 118
Khan, Hulagu 92
Khatami, Mohammad 183
Khayyam, Omar 90–91
Khomeini, Ayatollah Ruhollah 120

King, Mervyn 150
King David Schools 82
Kissinger, Henry 119, 137
Klein, Naomi 113
Knight Rider 185
knowledge 77, 85-7, 103-4, 211
Kurds 113, 119–20, 130
Kuwait 112

Lancashire, Pakistani community 21–3
land ownership 138–9
language 105
Latin America 117, 137–41
Lebanon 111, 124, 126
Leonardo da Vinci 97
libraries 86, 93
Libya 114
life, origins of 72–5
Life on Mars 19–20
light 78, 97
Lincoln, Abraham 147
Lions for Lambs 188
Liverpool 32-5, 37, 41, 53-4, 82, 180–81, 186, 212

Maimonides, Moses 95, 104
Malaysia 103, 183
Manchester University 47-53
Manji, Irshad 172–8, 200
Maragheh 86, 92
marriage, forced 201
materialism 15, 190
mathematics 87–91
Maude, General F. S. 113
measles 95
Mecca, pilgrimage to (Hajj) 165, 169–70
media 11, 52, 153-4

negativity about Islam 11,
 162–5, 171–2, 192, 202
medicine 86, 94–101
Merseyside Council of Faiths 212
Miami Vice 185
military expenditure 76, 113, 124,
 136, 152, 154
Milky Way 69, 93
Miller, Stanley 73
miners' strike 153
mini-cabbing 26–7, 34
molecules 71–2
money lending 146–8, 156–8
Mongols 92, 131
Monroy, Carlos Julio Arosemena
 140
morality 210–11
Morocco 111
mosques 30–31, 33, 50–51
Mossadeq, Mohammad 117, 141
MPs' expenses scandal 190
Mubarak, Hosni 121
Muhammad (the Prophet) 13,
 77-8, 84, 163, 175, 178, 194, 201,
 203, 205
Muhammad, Younus 204
Mujahideen 35, 135
mullahs 76
Murray, Craig 207
music 195–6
Muslim Council of Britain 207
Muslim students 49–50
Muslims
 'moderate' 13–14
 'normal' 161, 164–5
myths 14

Nasser, Gamal Abdel 118
National Front 29

Nehru, Jawaharlal 128
Nelson, Lancashire 21, 27–8
newspapers see media
Nicaragua 139
niqab 30
Nixon, Richard 119, 137
Non-Aligned Movement 119
Nuclear Non-Proliferation Treaty
 127
nuclear weapons 124, 127, 129
numerals 85, 87, 88, 104

Obama, Barack 121
obesity 153
obstetrics 96
oil 30, 114, 116–18, 140
OPEC 118
Ottoman Empire 111

'Paki-bashing' 29
Pakistan 21–3, 48
 American interventions in
  121–3
 support for United States 128
 treatment by the West 123,
  127–9
Palestinians 125–6, 130, 178
papermaking 85
Paris 9–10
parties 44
Persian Empire 87
pharmacology 98
physics 70–72
Pinochet, General Augusto 137–8
political correctness 43–4
Pope Urban II 108, 110
poverty 160
prayer 31, 37
 times of day 165–9

pregnancy 96
privatisation 149
The Professionals 19
propaganda 154
protectionism 151
Ptolemy, Claudius 89, 92–3
public speaking 45–6, 58
public spending 148
pubs 44
pulmonary circulation 100–102
Punjab 23

Quilliam 180–1, 200
Quran 14–16, 30–31, 56, 62–4, 97,
  109, 131, 193–4
  as a divine work 62–3, 76–8
  on economic issues 141, 154–9
  on prayer times 166–7
  relevance to modern life
    165–72, 176–7, 196–200
  and science 62–3, 78
  urges search for knowledge 85,
    87, 91
  on usury 156–8

racism 43, 202, 210
radicalisation 59, 83
Rafiq, Haris 206
Ramadan 165, 168–9
Ramadan, Tariq 177, 182, 198
rap music 195
Reagan, Ronald 139
reason 61–4, 67, 193
regime change 137
religion, seen as irrational 61–7
Renaissance 83-4, 177
Rendition 188
Revolution Muslim 203–5
Richard the Lionheart 110

Roman Catholicism 66
Romero, Archbishop Oscar
139–40
Rushdie, Salman 51

Saeed, Abdullah 176–7
Saladin 109–10
Sardar, Zia 35–6
The Satanic Verses 51, 53
Saudi Arabia 38
Scandinavia 166
scholars 76–7, 86
science 62–3, 66–79, 82-3, 87, 103
Servetus, Michael 101
sexual exploitation 202
Shahak, Israel 124, 127
Shakespeare, William 81
Shamir, Yitzhak 126
Shariah law 35
Sharif, Mohammed 26–9
Sharon, Ariel 126
The Shock Doctrine 113
Sikhism 28
Sind ibn Ali 87–8
slavery 153
smoking 27, 153, 198
socialism 142
solar system 68–70
soul 65
South Park 203–4
Soviet Union 128, 136
space 68–70
Starsky and Hutch 185
stress 142
subsidies 152–3
Sufism 205–7
Suharto, General (later President)
  119
Sukarno, President 118–19, 141

Sunni Muslims 119
surgery 95
The Sweeney 19
Syria 114
Syriana 188

Taliban 123, 135
talks 13, 58
teachers 42
telepathy 68
television 19–20, 34, 37, 185, 188, 190
Thatcher, Margaret 135
tolerance 109, 129–30
Toyota 20
trigonometry 90
tuberculosis 23
Tunisia 111, 114
Turkey 103, 183

UK Islamic Mission 38
ulema 76–7
unemployment 11, 159
United Fruit Company 138–9
United Nations 127, 128
universe 68–70
university 47, 48–53, 61–2, 86
Urdu 45
usury 146–8, 156–8

values 76, 190
Venezuela 141
Vesalius, Andreas 101–102
violence 26, 34, 38, 195

Wadud, Amina 177, 182
Wahhabi network 38
War on Terror 121
Watson, Phil 42–3

welfare state 151
The West Wing 188
Western culture
  dominance 80–81
  Islamic influence 84–106
  problems of 141–54
  women 37, 49, 66, 174, 177, 182, 195-6, 200–201
World Bank 149
World Trade Organisation 149, 152

Yerrakadu, Andrew 52–4, 186
Yorkshire 29
youth camps 59–60

zakat 155–6
Zaman Khan, Dr Ahmed 35–7
zero 88, 89, 105
Zia, General 35
Zionism 204

Zia Chaudhry's family originally came from Pakistan, and he was brought up in Liverpool. After graduating from Manchester University, he was called to the Bar in 1991. In the last decade he has become increasingly involved in inter-faith dialogue, and has addressed a variety of audiences, including the judiciary, school pupils, criminal offenders and assorted Church groups. He featured in the ITV series *Soul to Soul* hosted by Jo Brand, and has made numerous radio appearances discussing Islam and related issues.